PRAISE & WORSHIP

2nd Printing

BY BISHOP E. BERNARD JORDAN

Praise and Worship
By Bishop E. Bernard Jordan

2nd Printing

PRAISE & WORSHIP is dedicated to my son, Joshua Nathaniel Jordan, for he has been anointed as a minstrel in the House of the Lord, and the spirit of Chenaniah shall rest upon him in his generation.

Alexander, Sylvester & Roxana

Beauty for Ashes Women's Ministries

Bell, Angela

Bernateau, Jacqeline

Bradford, George & Belinda

Burke, Sandra

Burnett, Lorena

Connor, Pastor Dorothy

Downs, Frankie

Eady, Karen

Eberiga, Pastors Richard & Diane

Edwards, Delores

Ellison Edwina,

Evans, Blanche

Harris, Maria A.

Jefferson, Robin

Johnson, Barbara

Johnson, Pastor Dolly M. &
    Passaic Christian Church

Jordan, Mother Mary

Khuri, Terry

Manton, Thomas K.

Marocik, Ferenc

Marocik, Katalin

Marocik, Marika

Marocik, Robert

Mellette, Pastor Charles

Miles, Pastor Connie

Morris, Diane

Murray, Alice M.

Nelson, Darlene

Nelson, Doris

New Life Ministries, Inc.

Queen, Maria

Reid, Marshah

Rhodes, Sonshine F.M.

Ricks, Pastor Carolyn

Robinson, David & Angela

Savery, Harlene

Simmons, Delmus

Stanley, Rosalind

Sutton, Rev. Talmadge

Tucker, Olivia

Tutt-Beckford, Yolanda

Vasquez, Jorge I.

Ward, Gwendolyn

Westley, Tony & Ina Pastors

Wilkinson, Pastors Theodore
    & Arthurine

Because of their generosity and obedience to the Spirit of God, we know that they have opened the door for miracles, and we believe that He shall cause the gems of wisdom that are contained in these pages to be made manifest in each of their lives, for the reward of the Lord is sure and addeth no sorrow!

In His Love and Service,
Bishop E. Bernard & Debra Jordan

The highest calling that we possess as members of the Body of Christ is to express ourselves in worship at the feet of Jesus. The innate ability to respond to the love and compassion of our Heavenly Father deserves to be understood and cultivated in our lives. Worship is the expression of our reverence for an Omniscient, Omnipotent and Omnipresent God who made us in His Image with a capacity to identify with Him. When we stop to think of the awesomeness of God; the utter magnitude of His Essence, we find ourselves overcome like the psalmist David, who asked, "What is man, that Thou art mindful of him?"

Yet we find that God made man with His purpose in mind, and loved us enough to allow His Son, Jesus, to die in our stead, that we would then have access to communion with Him.

To render praise unto the Lord is a calling of the highest order, and one which each of us should take great pleasure in fulfilling. To extol His majesty and glorify His Name in the earth is more than a vocalization... it is a lifestyle that will bestow honor upon Whom honor is due. It is a life which has been dedicated and sanctified; separated from mediocrity and marked by the excellence of God that well demonstrate the veneration which is rendered unto Him.

PRAISE and WORSHIP has been written to challenge and inspire those who are called as psalmists and minstrels in the House of the Lord, as well as those who desire a deeper understanding and freedom in their times of personal worship. The Spirit of the Lord invites you to intimacy... to get to know Him, for He is multifaceted, and will be to you what you will allow Him to be.

TABLE OF CONTENTS

CHAPTER 1

The 39 books of the Old Testament can be put into five major divisions as follows:

1.   FIVE books of Law or Pentateuch (Genesis to Deuteronomy)

2.   TWELVE books of History (Joshua to Esther)

3.   FIVE books of Poetry (Job to Song of Solomon)

4.   FIVE books of Major Prophets (Isaiah to Daniel)

5.   TWELVE books of Minor Prophets (Hosea to Malachi)

In many books and biblical literary studies these categories are commonly used. They describe in a general way the major content of the books. In our study we will divide the books into larger categories. The Books of Law and History, books dealing with God's plan and specific direction for man's life on earth. The creation and fall of man, the raising up of a chosen nation, the interaction between God and His people. The Books of the Prophets, these are books dealing with God's continual direction of man to do His purposes. The thoughts and plan of God being revealed as they are and will unfold from age to age. The Books of Poetry, books containing a variety of songs, laments, and praises. Proverbs is a book of condensed truth that releases the wisdom of God in man when applied. The Psalms are a hymnal for man dealing with God's glory, power, and goodness as recognized through man's continual praise and worship of Him.

THE PSALMS

Psalms in the Greek is spelled, "Psalmos," according to Vine's Expository Dictionary of New Testament Words. Psalmos primarily denotes striking or twitching with the fingers on musical "strings; a sacred Psalmos sung to musical accompaniment. "The Psalms" are used often in the Old Testament and New Testament. In Luke 20, verses 42-43, we read:

"And David himself saith in the book of Psalms, The Lord said unto my Lord, Sit thou on my right hand, Till I make thine enemies thy footstool."

Therefore, we can see that the book of Psalms was a prophetic book that had seemingly given many Messianic prophecies. Also, as we begin to look in the book of Psalms according to Acts chapter 1, verse 20, when referring to Judas it says:

"For it is written in the book of Psalms, Let his habitation be desolate, and let no man dwell therein: and his bishopric let another take."

The Psalms was very much a book that was used in the New Testament Church and it is still a vital book in the church today. Jesus seemingly made this distinction when He said, in Luke 24 we read:

".... These are the words which I spake unto you, while I was yet with you, that all things must be fulfilled, which were written in the law of Moses, and in the prophets, and in the psalms concerning me."

To say that the Psalms was a book that was under the Law would be erroneous. It would, therefore, seem that the Psalms had a total distinction from the Law. the Psalms is a New Testament book as well. In Colossians 3, verse 16, we read:

"Let the word of Christ dwell in you richly in all wisdom; teaching and admonishing one another in psalms and hymns and spiritual songs, singing with grace in your hearts to the Lord."

There is very good reason to believe that the Psalms served as the songbook of the Early Church, and the Church today.

WHAT IS PRAISE AND WORSHIP?

"PRAISE" Often praise and thanksgiving go hand in hand. They are closely related, yet their meanings are slightly different. Thanksgiving arises from our need to show appreciation for the goodness of God and for the gifts He bestows upon us. I thank God for my home, my healthy child, my good job, the beauty of a rose, a sunny day, and a gentle spring rain, etc. Praise stems from the desire to love and to extol God for who He is, rather than for what He does. I praise God for being all powerful, all good, all truth, and all knowing. I praise God because of who He is.

In spite of the appearances and circumstances of my life and in spite of my financial situation, I can look up and tell God, "I praise You." I know that You are "Jehovah Jireh." I know that You are the One who will see to it that every one of my needs are provided. I praise You because I know that You are "Jehovah Tsidkenu," the Lord our Righteousness and I can praise You for that. I praise You in spite of what I might be feeling in my natural body, for You are "Jehovah Rapha," "the Lord our God who heals us." Our praise does not stem from what God has done, but our praise comes from who He is.

In a sense, we really won't know what it is to praise God until we praise Him in the midst of the last thing we wish to do.

We may feel that God hasn't answered our prayers or performed as quickly as we felt He should. There's a song that is sung in some Pentecostal churches that goes: "He may not come when you want Him, but He's right on time!" How often we have experienced the truth of that!

There was a time that I felt that God should break in immediately, and He didn't do it! During that time and season of waiting, God commanded me to praise Him despite how I felt.

"WORSHIP" In Hebrews, the word worship means "to bow oneself down in adoration and contemplation of God." Worship involves devotion, reverence, adoration, respect, and honor. My wife and I once began a service by telling those present to bow down before the Lord and throw Him a kiss. What followed was beautiful! Everyone in the congregation bowed and threw the Master a kiss and the Holy Spirit expressed the heart of the Father. In Matthew 4, verse 10, we read:

> *"Thou shalt worship the Lord thy God, and him only shalt thou serve."*

Therefore, if you want to receive from God you must worship God and Him alone. To whom you render worship will determine from whom you will receive. He will give to you as you begin to worship Him. God wants us to arrive at a place where as we bow before Him, it will not be just the bowing down of the outer man, but the bowing down or bending of our hearts (inner man).

I saw an amazing illustration of a human heart. Viewed at a specific angle, the heart appeared to be bowing down. That is how our spirit should be as we humbly bow down in the Presence of God.

Humility is an interesting thing. Sometimes, we can have pride in our humility. I recall an incident at a large conference where a speaker announced his disappointment with the offering for the amount that he had expected hadn't been given. Almost immediately a sister came forward and brought forth a word saying that there was sin in the speaker's life. It was a sin about his pride in his faith. All this happened in front of thousands of people.

Often, an individual can begin to become prideful and try to do things in their own, strength leaving God on the outside. We must always make sure, as we begin to move in the things of God, that we always maintain our faith in God. To have faith in our ability alone will cause us to move outside of Christ. Therefore, we must make sure we are always moving in a corporate mentality - trusting and believing God and looking to Him instead of looking unto ourselves as the final turning point, for that will make things happen.

Now, the speaker didn't get his request because he relied solely upon his faith and not upon the faith of those present. It was time for the Body of Christ, those present at the meeting, to add their faith to his for every joint was called to supply. Because of one man's pride in his faith, God would not grant the request.

COMING INTO PRAISE AND WORSHIP

We need to be reminded that the praise and worship service in our churches are not meant to be just an "interlude" or a time to wait for latecomers. The song service is a necessity! It is a time of preparation where those present prepare the ground of their heart for the successful planting of the seed of the Word. In Psalms 100, verses 1-2, we read:

> *"Make a joyful noise unto the Lord, all ye lands! Serve the Lord with gladness! Come before his presence with singing."*

Notice it doesn't say, "Serve the Lord with sadness." We are to come into the Presence of God with singing! In Psalms 100, verses 3-4, we read:

> *"Know ye that the Lord he is God, it is he that hath made us, and not we ourselves; we are his people and the sheep of his pasture. Enter into his gates with thanksgiving, and into his courts with praise, be thankful unto him, and bless his name."*

When we come into the Lord's Presence in prayer, we are not to come saying, "My name is Jimmy, so gimme, gimme, gimme!" We need to come into God's Presence with thanksgiving. "I thank you Lord for waking me up this morning."

When you go in to see the King, you should enter singing praises to Him. Even in our earthly realm, when people go into the King's Presence, they go in proclaiming his goodness and praising him. So when we come into the Presence of the King of kings and Lord of lords, we come into His court singing and speaking His praises. When Jesus gave His disciples the example of prayer in Matthew chapter 6, He said, "Our Father which art in heaven," which acknowledges God as Father. The next thing He said was "Hallowed be Thy Name," which is praise. Praise precedes petition. Before Jesus mentioned the petitionary aspect of prayer, (making request), He instructed His disciples that they were to offer praise first by saying, "Hallowed be Thy Name." "Hallowed" means "Holy." In other words, "Holy is Thy Name." We must come to the realization that our God is Holy. In Psalms 100, verse 4-5, we read:

> "...... Be thankful unto him, and bless his name. For the Lord is good; his mercy is everlasting; and his truth endureth to all generations."

The truth of God endures forever. Here the word truth is "Emunah." According to the Theological Word Book of the Old Testament, Emunah is defined as "fullness" or "faithfulness." We see that it is talking about the faithfulness of God as illustrated in Exodus. In Exodus 17, verse 12, we read:

> "But Moses hands were heavy and they took a stone, and put it under him, and he sat thereon; and Aaron and Hur stayed up his hands, the one on the one side, and the other on the other side; and his hands were steady until the going down of the sun."

The word truth denotes that one of the attributes of God is faithfulness or dependableness. This is a key to understanding the divine attributes of God. You can depend on Him. You can look to Him to be faithful. He is steadfast. There is no variableness nor shadow of turning in Him because He is a dependable God.

THE IMPORTANCE OF PRAISE AND WORSHIP

Today the Body of Christ is being reminded anew of the importance of worship and the importance of praise. In the early 1980's we were reminded of the importance of intercession. The Church is always being reminded of the importance of a particular truth. Almost every time God begins to restore a truth in the Body of Christ, there are those who will take that truth to an extreme. They will elevate that truth to such a high place that they put all other truths below it, and then a whole church or ministry evolves out of it.

God established some truths concerning the importance of the ministry of helps. Certain churches really started emphasizing the "ministry of helps." Everything you heard concerned "helps ministry." People began to fight to strive to attain a place in the "helps ministry." Most of them didn't recognize that they weren't anointed for that purpose by God. There is a difference between a person who is called into a ministry such as helps, and someone who is part of the ministry. A person called into the ministry of helps is anointed with the wisdom of God to know how to help and how to get things done. The leaders don't always have to tell that person what to do. They are anointed by the Spirit to know how to put things forth so that they work. A helper, on the other hand, may mean well and want to do something, but he or she may occasionally get in the way.

A few years later, in the mid-1980's, there was a great emphasis on intercession. Churches and groups began developing many teachings and activities that emphasized intercession. Some people left their original churches and formed churches and ministries based primarily on intercession.

Most definitely, intercessory prayer has its importance in the Body of Christ, but the Church will not be perfected through prayer. In Ephesians chapter 4, verses 11-12, we read:

"And he gave some, apostles; and some, prophets; and some, evangelists; and some, pastors and teachers; For the perfecting of the saints, for the work of the ministry, for the edifying of the body of Christ."

This is how the church comes into perfection. The word "perfection" means "maturity through the governmental gifts that God has set in the church." Even if a person prays 10 hours a day, 365 days a year, he or she will still need to sit under the ministry of the Word of God in order to be perfected. Prayer is just a part. We must make sure that we don't take the part and make it the whole.

THE DANGER OF MAKING THE PART THE WHOLE

Let's consider the danger of taking the part and making it the whole.

On one pitch dark night, three people that were walking in the jungle came upon an elephant. They didn't have any lights, and they began feeling around in the dark and touching different parts of the elephant, trying to understand what it was. The first person took hold of the elephant's legs and said, "This is a pillar." The second person felt along the elephant's trunk and said, "This is a fire hose." The third person touched the elephant's tusk and said, "This is a large bone."

Notice how each person took the part of the elephant that they were touching and used it alone to try to identify the whole object in front of them. They each made an erroneous judgement. Not one of them came close to identifying the true identify of the elephant. That is the type of thing that happens when we, the Body of Christ, take part of a truth or doctrine and try to make it the whole.

It is vital to know that we need each other. Those three people might have identified the elephant if they had combined and discussed all their information. As the church, we will never walk in the entire truth of the land. We must properly fit the pieces of the truth that we each comprehend. By doing this we will bring it into the pool of larger truth.

There is a part of God which you have that I don't have. I need it. I need you to impart it me. There is something you've experienced that I haven't experienced. I need to hear about that, and you need to hear the part that I can contribute. When we begin to learn the importance and the value of covenant, we'll find that we cannot just hold on to our part and make it the whole. We all need our part and the part of everyone else to get the whole picture of what God is saying and doing.

GOD AND WORSHIP

Let's consider Psalms 22 and study an aspect of praise (verse 1).

"My God, my God, why hast thou forsaken me? Why art thou so far from helping me, and from the words of my roaring?"

This was a prayer of the psalmist, but we also recognize the powerful work of Jesus on the cross. As He cried out, "My God, My God, why hast thou forsaken me," we believe it was then that Jesus became sin for us. How do we know this? There is no place else in the Bible where Jesus addressed His Father as "God." Elsewhere, He always addressed Him as "Father." Clearly, God can never be the Father of the sinner. He can only be the Father of the righteous. Jesus became a sin offering - and took the sins of the world upon His Body on the cross. He therefore, called out, "My God, My God."

In Psalms 22 verses 2 and 3 we read:

"O my God, I cry in the daytime, but thou hearest not; and in the night season, and am not silent. But thou art holy, O thou that inhabitest the praises of Israel."

God is the one who inhabits or lives in the praises of Israel. The word, "Israel" means "He will rule as God." When you are one who is ruling in the dominion that God has given you, He will live and dwell in the midst of your praise.

Another translation of verse 3 reads: "He is enthroned on the praises of Israel." God will take His seat and establish His throne upon our praise. That is why the devil tries to keep us from praising. That is also why God encourages us to praise. Every time I praise God, my hand is in the neck of the enemy.

Praise will still the enemy. The lack of praise will still the Hand of God. When I'm at home or when I'm walking down the street, I'll find myself raising my hands and exclaiming, "Glory to God." "Alleluia!" Sometimes I catch myself meditating on the goodness of the Lord, and I'll look up into the clouds and say, "Oh Lord, oh Lord, how excellent is Thy Name in all the earth. All that Thou has created shall declare Thy glory!"

I doubt that it is by chance the word "praise" contains the word "raise." I believe praise will raise us up and bring us out of our present circumstances into the glorious Presence of God. During times of oppression and depression, we must begin to praise the Lord. As we triumph through Jesus Christ, our hand reaches up and throttles the neck of our adversary.

QUESTIONS FOR REFLECTION

1. Think about some of the praise and worship services at your church. How have you regarded those services? How have most people in the congregation regarded them? Are there positive changes that might be made? Discuss.

2. Praise stems from a desire to extol God for Who He is. Who is God to you? Jot down a few ideas on paper. You might want to share them with a friend. Use your reflections to praise God more specifically in your daily prayer times.

3. Many church songs are based upon the Psalms. Locate several favorite songs and read the whole Psalm from which they are taken. If possible, locate several musical versions of the same Psalm.

4. Find a favorite or familiar Psalm. Try singing the word, using either a simple melody you make up or the tune of a familiar hymn. You can try doing this with a simple prayer of thanksgiving, also.

5. If you aren't already doing this, set aside 10 to 15 minutes very day for personal praise and worship. Do this for two weeks, despite how you feel. After the two weeks, notice the changes in your circumstances and attitudes. Make these prayer times a permanent part of your life.

CHAPTER 2

Just as there are dimensions of prayer, I believe there are dimensions of praise. Occasionally, I just don't feel like praising God, but I praise Him anyway. I use my will. I offer up the sacrifice of praise, despite how I feel.

We all need to get geared up for praise. We need to come into the House of the Lord with the attitude: "I'm coming today to praise the Lord." In some churches, the song leaders stand up front and act like cheerleaders. They motivate the congregation to share their excitement and enthusiasm. The people of God should learn to love praising the Lord on their own accord. The love of God should be their primary motivation.

My vision is to have a church where every musical instrument on the face of the earth - a full orchestra - is routinely playing at the worship services. I'm believing God for that. Even instruments that are not yet in the earth should be there for we'll create them after the pattern of God. Music is a ministry of expression before God, and is able to communicate and articulate the deepest feeling of the heart. It evokes man's response to God and in turn, God's response to man.

I believe that God wants to restore the creativity of the arts to the Body of Christ, and that the day is coming when we will see artists ministering in the House of the Lord. Artists will draw during the time of praise and worship, getting the mind of God and portraying the glory of God. The artwork in the House of the Lord should be done by those who are anointed, cunning and skillful. God is the best interior decorator!

We are going to see both men and women dancing before the Lord. David danced before the Lord. Even the priests had to be able to dance. They jumped and twirled in the air during worship. Psalms 69, verses 30 and 31 says:

"I will praise the name of God with a song, and will magnify him with thanksgiving. This also shall please the Lord ...."

If you want to please God, begin to praise Him. There's a time to come before the Lord saying, "Lord I love You, I praise You, I just bless Your Name."

Sometimes you'll leave that time of praise with the answer for some concern you had before you began praising. God will quicken the answer to your intellect.

"This also shall please the Lord better than an ox or bullock that hath horns and hoofs."
Psalms 69:31

Sacrifices were being offered, but the psalmist was letting them know that praise is better than sacrifice. God looks more at your praise than at the things you sacrifice, for the praise is coming right from your innermost being.

"The humble shall see this, and be glad: and your heart shall live that seek God."
Psalms 69:32

PRAISE - A SACRIFICE

In Hosea chapter 14 we read:

"O ISRAEL, return unto the Lord, thy God; for thou hast fallen by thine iniquity.
Take with you words, and turn to the LORD: say unto him, Take away all iniquity, and
receive us graciously: so will we render the calves of our lips. Asshur shall not save us;
we will not ride upon horses: neither will we say any more to the work of our hands. Ye
are our gods: for in thee the fatherless findeth mercy."

As the Israelites praised the Lord, they "render[ed] the calves" of their lips. In other words, praise was looked at as a sacrifice. Their lips offered unto God an acceptable sacrifice of praise.

THE WORKS OF OUR HANDS

According to Hosea, the Israelites no longer looked upon their hands as their gods. There are those who seem to believe that the mark of the beast which is mentioned in Revelation will be done by some sort of machine which will stamp out the numbers "666." They have gotten rid of things with numbers, such as their credit cards. However, I don't believe that is how things will happen. In fact, I see a danger here. We may get so busy looking for the antichrist that we don't look for Christ.

The book of Revelation is not a revelation of the antichrist, but it is the revelation of Jesus Christ, that He might be unveiled to all. I believe that the "mark of the beast" on people's hands and foreheads can definitely be referring to the effects of humanism. The number "6" is the mark of man. What humanism teaches and what humanists want is your mind and your hands. They want to dominate the works of your hands, and deny the existence of God by exalting the power of man.

We can do all things, but we do them through Christ Jesus. It is Christ who strengthens us and gives us the ability to do things. Those who will have the mark of satan will have humanism in their minds, and their hands will execute it through their refusal to arise and magnify God. That's why the Bible tells us that we need to renew our minds by the Word of God. As we do this, our minds will have the mark of God.

We are to come into the Presence of God with singing. God inhabits and lives in the midst of the praises of His people. Praise is pleasing to God, as it represents the fruit of our relationship with Him.

Hebrews chapter 13, verse 15 says:
> *"By him therefore let us offer the sacrifice of praise to God continually, that is, the fruit of our lips giving thanks to his name."*

What is the sacrifice we are told to offer here? It is the fruit of our lips that will render the beauty of praise. There is a Scripture in Psalms which says, *"Kiss the Son, lest he be angry ..."* (2:12). We need to kiss Him with the fruit of our lips.

PRAISE: A THOUGHT-FILLED ACT

Praise must be moved beyond the mere ritual of format. It's possible to say, "Praise the Lord" while our mind is on the Chinese food we're going to have after the church service. We need to progress to a degree where our minds are continually on Him. We must enter praise having awareness of Who we are praising.
Verse 1 of Psalms 45 says:
> *"My heart is inditing a good matter: I speak of the things which I have made touching the king: my tongue is the pen of a ready writer."*

The word "inditing" means to "express or describe in prose or verse; to compare and write." Our hearts are to be continually comparing the praise of God, and our tongues are to pronounce the meditation therein. Our tongues are inscribing the nature of our relationship with the Lord. We are giving unto the Lord the message of our hearts.

"Lord, let me look at the matters, sum them up and give unto You a statement."

In Ephesians, we read: *"For we are his workmanship ..." (2:10).* The Greek word for "workmanship" is "poiema," which means "poem." We are the poem, the statement of the Lord. God has spoken His Word concerning our lives. We are each a statement walking in the earth. When people see our lives, they see a poem.

Every time I come before the Lord, my heart speaks of the handwork of God and adoration in praise. It is that statement or poem which is ascending into the Father's nostrils as a sweet smelling incense before Him. Each of us are to be a prophetic similitude of the reality of Christ in the earth. When people see us, they should see Jesus. They should see Christ in us - the Hope of Glory! Our prayer should be, "Lord, make my life in such a way that the statement which You are speaking to earth through the book of my life will be clearly read of men. For I am your workmanship. I am the poem of the Lord." Psalms 45 continues in verse 11:

"So shall the king greatly desire thy beauty: for he is thy Lord; and worship thou him."

And in Psalms 86 we read:

"All nations whom thou hast made shall come and worship before thee, O Lord; and shall glorify thy name." (verse 9).

The book of Psalms is a Kingdom book. It lets us know that every nation, and every culture and every kingdom in the world will join the heavenly processional and worship the Lord. They will stand before God in the uniqueness of their various expressions and magnify Him in the beauty of holiness.

There are many people who are looking for God's Kingdom in the future. They eagerly await Jesus' immediate return to the earth. The Scriptures tell us that we are reigning with Him NOW. We are seated in heavenly places with Christ Jesus (Ephesians 2:6). Many are looking for His thousand year reign. One brother in the Lord described what is happening in terms of an exciting program: Jesus was born, died, rose and ascended into the heavenlies - then there's a long commercial break during which time generations of people are waiting for Jesus to come back. In his view, the church is presently, more or less, standing still in a kind of "commercial break," waiting for the day when those in the Church of God will be snatched out of this world.

The Bible does not bear witness to the "television story" as described above. In fact, it says that the Kingdom of God is at hand. It is here and now. The psalmist tells us that ALL OF THE NATIONS shall come and worship the Lord.
Psalms 95, verse 6 and 7, says:

"O come, let us worship and bow down: let us kneel before the Lord our maker. For he is our God ..."

God desires us to worship Him. Russia, China, Haiti, England, the United States - every kingdom and nation is going to come and worship God as King of kings and Lord of lords. This won't occur because of any nation's form of governmen, for all will be done under the government of God.

WORSHIP OF GOD ALONE

After satan invited Jesus to worship him in exchange for all the world's kingdoms, Then saith Jesus unto him, "Get thee hence, Satan: for it is written, Thou shalt worship the Lord thy God, and him only shalt thou serve." (Matthew 4:10). Satan wanted Jesus' worship. He understood clearly the importance and power of worship. Jesus refused to worship him.

We must make certain that we do not allow our focus to swerve off Almighty God and settle on a man, causing our worship to be man-centered, rather than God-centered. This is the sin of idolatry, which places man on a pedestal that was only meant to be occupied by God. Great men and women have left the Christian scene because people began to worship and make a "god" out of them. There were many such idols created in the 1950's and '60's. They cannot be identified today because when they died or left their particular ministries, the movements centered around them ended, which was the judgement of a jealous God.

PRAISE - A WAY TO DELIVERANCE

When we truly understand that praise is essential in our lives, we're going to see changes manifest among us. In Genesis chapter 49, verse 8, we read:

"Judah, thou art he whom thy brethren shall praise: thy hand shall be in the neck of thine enemies ..."

We know that the word "Judah" means "praise." If we are going to be the "Judah" of God, we are going to have to be the Praise of God. When Adam walked with God in the cool of the day, he walked praising the Lord. We need to come into His Presence and just love Him for Who He is.

Meditate on the goodness of the Lord. "Lord, I thank you for Who You are. I just want to praise You." When praise begins to ring out of our temple, it will touch the throne of God. We shall see God coming down, dwelling in the midst of us. He will inhabit the praises of His people. He will inhabit your praises.

QUESTIONS FOR REFLECTION

1. What are some specific things you can do to make your personal and corporate praise more thought-filled? Do several of these things and see how they affect your personal and corporate praise and worship.

2. List the dimensions of praise mentioned in this chapter. Which one is least familiar to you? Discuss that dimension of praise and think of ways it might be used in your personal or church praise and worship.

3. "When people see our lives, they see a poem. They see a statement of God." Do you know people whose lives are a statement of God? How is this true of your life? Begin to thank God for making your life His statement.

4. List three teachings of humanism with which you are personally familiar. Look up scriptures that specifically come against these teachings. Then do any or all of the following: (a) Write out one of the Scriptures. Post it in a prominent spot in your home. Memorize it. (b) Make a simple poster or banner based on one of the Scriptures. Display it in your home and/or in your church hall. (c) Find a song based on one of the Scriptures. Sing it as you worship the Lord in your home and/or at church.

STUDY QUESTIONS

1. The people of God should learn to love _____ the Lord.
2. God wants to restore _____ to the Body of Christ.
3. _____ danced before the Lord. Even He had to be able to dance.
4. Praise is better than _____.
5. The book of Revelation is not the revelation of the _____ , but the revelation of Jesus Christ.
6. What humanism teaches and what the humanist wants is your mind and your _____.
7. We need to progress to where our praise is to such a degree that our _____ are continually on _____.
8. The Greek word for workmanship is poiema, which means "_____ ."
9. _____ is at hand. It is here and now.
10. If we are going to be the Judah of God, we are going to have to be the _____.

CHAPTER 3

THE VALUE OF WORSHIP

Satan realizes the value and importance of worship. When Jesus was in the wilderness, satan offered Him all the kingdoms of the world. The only condition was that Jesus must worship him. In Matthew 4, verses 8-9, we read:

> *"Again, the devil taketh him up into an exceeding high mountain, and sheweth him all the kingdoms of the world, and the glory of them; And saith unto him, All these things will I give thee, if thou wilt fall down and worship me."*

Satan wanted Jesus to worship him because worship implies that the person or object being worshiped is esteemed greater than the worshipper. If Jesus would have worshiped him it would have added credence to satan's ambition to be like God. If satan had succeeded in acquiring worship from Jesus then the entire plan of salvation would have been aborted, and satan would have a legal right to be named the god of this world. "Then saith Jesus unto him, 'Get thee hence, Satan: for it is written, Thou shalt worship the Lord thy God, and him only shalt thou serve.'" (verse 10). All the kingdoms of the world are going to worship the Lord, no matter how it may now appear in the natural. God's Kingdom will come!

God is doing a tremendous restoration of His people and His Church. He is raising up a people of balance who will move in His counsel and display what God wants to be revealed in this day. The Church of the Living God is to be a glorious Church without spot or wrinkle. This kind of Church will only come forth under the authority of the Word of God. We are going to see the liberty of the Holy Ghost in this day in such a way that the world is going to take notice that there is a people in the earth who represent the Kingdom of God.

PRAISE AND INTERCESSION

Revelation chapter 8, verse 1, records the Lord's opening of the seventh seal and the sending forth of the angels.

"And when he had opened the seventh seal, there was silence in heaven about the space of half an hour."

Note that seven is the number of completion and perfection. (An excellent book for those interested in studying Biblical Numerology is "Numbers in Scriptures, by Bullinger.) The Lord created the world in six days and on the seventh day He rested. The complete scale on a musical keyboard is seven notes. There are seven colors in a rainbow.

With the opening of that seventh seal there was silence in Heaven for half an hour. This is unusual, for normally Heaven is a noisy place filled with singing and the blaring of trumpets.

In Revelation, chapter 8, verses 2-3 we read:

"And I saw the seven angels which stood before God; and to them were given seven trumpets. And another angel came and stood at the altar, having a golden censer; and there was given unto him much incense, that he should offer it with the prayers of all saints upon the golden altar which was before the throne."

Incense represents praise, prayer, and worship. Everything is connected. There is a difference between the prayer of petition and the prayer of praise. The prayer of petition is asking God to act on a matter, while the prayer of praise says, "God, I'm going to praise you no matter what, in spite of the circumstances, for all things are in Your Hands. You are the great "I AM." (Exodus 3:14.) "I AM" will be unto me just what I need Him to be for He is the "I AM." Before moving beyond the veil into the Holy of Holies, a priest had to go to the altar of incense. The incense was an odor sent up to the nostrils of the Father.

In Psalms 141, verses 1-2, we read:

"LORD, I cry unto thee: make haste unto me; give ear unto my voice, when I cry unto thee. Let my prayer be set forth before thee as incense ..."

In the Tabernacle of Moses, the thing that stood before the veil was the altar of incense. The book of Revelation speaks of praise going up before the Father making intercession for us. It is a people of praise who will bring forth the Kingdom of God in the dimension destined of Him.

In Revelation chapter 8, verse 4, we read:

> "*And the smoke of the incense which came with the prayers of the saints, ascended up before God out of the angel's hand.*"

As the incense ascends upwards before God, it becomes mingled with the prayers of the saints. True prayer is only that which is lit by the fire of God. True prayer is that which the Lord is speaking and that which He is directing to be uttered.

There is a type of prayer sanctioned by a person's soul. "Lord, get me out of this situation right now!" This is vastly different from a prayer unctioned by the Spirit of God.

A few years ago, my daughter begged to accompany me to the store. She enjoyed the shopping at first, but after two hours she became tired, hot, and uncomfortable. She began tugging on my arm saying, "Daddy, I want to go now." She stopped a few minutes, but was soon back again, "Daddy, I want to go home." This happened at least ten times. All of a sudden I felt the Holy Spirit quicken me. He said, "That's the way you act when you say to me, "Lord Jesus, I don't like this situation I'm in right now. Get me out of this! Take it away!"

Do you realize that we often sing songs in church about "wanting to get out of this world" and we're "leaving the earth to go up to Heaven to get our reward?" One song most people will recognize instantly is "Swing Low, Sweet Chariot." There are many others! The truth is, none of us are going to Heaven to get a reward. Jesus said, "I come quickly. My reward is with Me." True prayer begins when we say, "*Lord, not my will, but Your will...Father, Thy Kingdom come, on earth as it is in Heaven.*"

BRINGING FORTH GOD'S KINGDOM

According to the Pulpit Commentary, Joshua 10:13 and II Samuel 1:18 refers to a book of war that the Israelites had which seems to have been the book of Jasher. They regarded praise as their weapon. It was an instrument of war and not just adoration. There were times when the Israelites went out with praise, and they had war on their minds.

The people of God will take the Kingdom. The Scripture tells us that "The Kingdom of God suffers violence and the violent take it by force" (see Matthew 11:12). We are to move in the force and power of God in such a degree that we take the Kingdom of God for His glory.

Many Christians know the Scripture says, "turn the other cheek," however, the Lord has clearly shown me that my suffering, of itself, is not of value to Him. It is one thing to truly suffer for the sake of the Kingdom, but there is also a time to pick up a stone and launch it at the head of the giant.

Jesus Christ went into the Temple, whipped those that cheated the people, released the animals, overturned the tables, and turned the whole Temple right side up. If He were to do that today in the church, many would object and say, "He's not walking in love." Yet, He was the love of God in action.

We are to teach our children how to behave in God's house. Some people in the world tell us never to discipline our children, instead, just be nice to them. The Biblical pattern says, "The rod of correction will drive out all foolishness" (Proverbs 22:15). That's the pattern of God. It's a pattern that, if followed wisely and faithfully, will eliminate many problems.

Are we to tolerate children hitting their parents, answering them back, and rudely questioning their authority? Certainly not. Children must be instantly corrected. The Lord has shown me that we cannot expect to deal with the children out on the streets until we have dealt with the children within our own homes and houses of worship. As parents and pastors, we are to display to our children the glory and authority of God.

This need for concern and vigilance is not new. Paul instructed Timothy that it was necessary to even teach adults how to behave in God's house.

We must be fully persuaded and convinced concerning the Kingdom of God. When we see anything that stands in the way of God's Kingdom, we must know it is to be removed and destroyed. How does all this go along with praise and worship? Praise will annihilate the works of the enemy. As we continue our study, we will see that praise and worship are literal and essential weapons of our warfare within our churches, in our homes, and out on the streets.

STUDY QUESTIONS CHAPTER 3

1. Satan realizes the _____ and _____ of worship.

2. _____ is the number of completion and perfection.

3. _____ represents praise, prayer, and worship.

4. There is a difference between the prayer of _____ and _____ the prayer of _____.

5. True _____ is only that which is lit by the fire of God.

6. There is a kind of prayer unction by a person's _____ .

7. Jesus said, "I come quickly. My_____ is with _____ ."

8. We are to move in the_____ and _____ of God to _____ such a degree that we take the Kingdom of God for His glory.

9. As parents and pastors, we are to display to our _____ the glory and authority of God.

10. _____ will annihilate the work of the enemy.

CHAPTER 4

KNOWING THE ORDER OF GOD

Have you ever been around a helpful four year old in a kitchen? He wants to help wash dishes or put away the plates but, of course, he doesn't know how. We hover around him trying to prevent accidents, such as broken china or spilling dish water all over the floor.

Too many adults in the Body of Christ are like that four year old. They want to help in the work of God, but they don't know how. Consequently, they are more often in the way than a help.

We need to understand the order of God. We are to move only with God's order and His purpose. We are to pray only those things unctioned by the Holy Spirit. Prayer unctioned by the Spirit is a sweet smelling savor in the Father's nostrils, but there is even more to it than that.

In Revelation, chapter 8, verses 4-5 we read:
> "*And the smoke of the incense, which came with the prayers of the saints, ascended up before God out of the angel's hand. And the angel took the censer, and filled it with fire of the altar, and cast it into the earth: and there were voices, and thunderings, and lightnings, and an earthquake.*"

Notice here, the Lord accepts the prayer and casts it back. That's why we read, "My word ... shall not return unto Me void" (Isaiah 55:11). Words unctioned by the Holy

Spirit, as they go up before the Father, will not return void, but will accomplish that which they have been sent out to do.

You may have been praying for years for the salvation of loved ones. Perhaps you need to move in a dimension of praising the Lord: "Lord, I thank you that they are coming into the Kingdom of God. I thank you for sending laborers to them. I praise you for what you are doing. Lord, I give you the glory that all my needs are met according to your riches and glory in Jesus Christ."

We ought to praise instead of complain! Certainly, we need to acknowledge when we have problems and difficulties. We are not to deny the reality of their existence, but we are to deny their right to remain. Also, we need to pray, recognizing our contact with the Answer, who is Jesus. In Him, all the promises of God are "yea and amen."

VAPORS AND THE CLOUD

The book of Job has often presented problems for some believers. Much damage has been done by the way this book has been traditionally preached and taught. We need to remember two things: everything in the Bible is truly stated. However, everything in the Bible is not a statement of truth.

In Job chapter 34 verse 35, we read:

"Job hath spoken without knowledge, and his words were without wisdom."

An example of this occurs in chapter 13, verse 15, when Job says, "Though he slay me, yet will I trust in him." We know that God does not slay His children. Job's sufferings were clearly an act of satan.

As we read conversations in Scripture, we need to be aware of who is making the statement. When Job was suffering, he didn't understand many things. He didn't realize who was sending the sufferings his way. Job spoke his own opinion and interpretation of his situation rather than God's. The Bible is true in telling us what Job said, but we are not to accept what Job said here as truth.

In Job chapter 36, verses 27-33, we read:

"For he maketh small the drops of water: they pour down rain according to the vapor thereof. Which the clouds do drop and distill upon man abundantly. Also can any understand the spreading of the clouds, or the noise of his tabernacle? Behold, he spreadeth his light upon it, and covereth the bottom of the sea. For by them judgeth he the people: he giveth meat in abundance. With clouds he covereth the light; and com-

mandeth it not to shine by the cloud that cometh betwixt. The noise thereof sheweth concerning it, the cattle also concerning the vapor."

Verse 27 tells us that God makes "small drops of water, and they pour down rain according to the vapor thereof." Do you realize that vapors ascend? As God drops the seed of His Word, and the thought of that Word goes into us, we need to release it and let it ascend back up to the Father. Let those vapors begin to arise! Let them take over and go into the clouds of God so that the clouds can begin to rain down on us again.

Worship is like vapors going up before the Father; prayer and praise is like vapors going up into the clouds. As the vapors ascend, the rain of God's clouds descend into our midst. We'll see the glory of God coming into manifestation as we "seed" the cloud of God with our praise and worship.

CLOUDS REPRESENT COVERING AND PROTECTION
As the Israelites traveled through the wilderness, God provided them with the cloud by day to protect them from the harsh rays of the sun, and the pillar of fire by night for light and warmth. As long as they remained under the cloud and by the fire, they were secure and safe.

Many who are traveling today have left the cloud. In some instances,the cloud has moved, and they've said, "Lord, I'm not ready to take that next journey." Such people are outside of the protection of God.

As we "seed" the cloud of God through worship and praise, we will experience God moving on our behalf. Prayer and praise create an atmosphere in which God can move.

"FORMULA" PRAISE
There are levels and degrees of praise. The bottom level of praise is done as a "method" or "formula." "Method" praise is two or three hymns mechanically sung at the beginning and/or ending of a Sunday morning service. Is praise done while waiting for a well-known person to begin ministering?

While singing, are we looking at our fingernails, reviewing our grocery shopping list or recalling details from a business conference last Friday? "Formula" praise is an abomination in the Father's nostrils. We need to guard against an attitude that says:

"Here we are on Sunday, doing this again." Let's all sing "This is the Day That the Lord Has Made," and "We Bring the Sacrifice of Praise." Meanwhile, our minds and our hearts are far away from God and His purposes.

Certainly, we need to consciously feel the Presence of God, yet we must guard against too much familiarity with God's Presence, for this would destroy a person in the end. The man who thought he could help God with the Ark of the Covenant became so familiar with God's Presence that it killed him (1 Chronicles 13:10). Note, it is possible for us to get so comfortable with God's Presence that we forget who He is. Also, it is easy for someone who feels comfortable with God to forget that He can still come down and judge us if we transgress against His pattern. He is the Architect. He is the Interior Decorator. Suppose you had a home custom designed and the construction company built your home according to different plans. Would you live in that home? Wouldn't you demand the builder make the adjustment according to the plans you gave him?

We may know God said to do something one way, but then we decide to cut expenses by doing it another way. God will say, "That's all right, you can do it that way, however, My glory won't be there. Many of us have done things with a substituted pattern where God's Presence was absent. We must follow the pattern of God.

In Zechariah chapter 14, verse 16-17, we read:
"And it shall come to pass, that every one that is left of all the nations which came against Jerusalem shall even go up from year to year to worship the King, the LORD of hosts, and to keep the feat of tabernacles. And it shall be, that whoso will not come up of all the families of the earth unto Jerusalem to worship the King, the LORD of hosts, even upon them shall be no rain."

See what happens if someone doesn't follow the pattern of God? "Even upon them shall be no rain." God told the Israelites to take their families to Jerusalem and those who didn't obey wouldn't have rain for the next year. Rain is vital for life. A person can live for forty days or perhaps a little more without food, but can only live for approximately two or three days without water.

CHURCH AFFILIATION
One sister who came to us for ministry was experiencing numerous problems. I happened to ask her where she worshiped. She responded, "Well, I go as the Spirit leads and directs me ..." I explained to her that she wasn't doing things according to God's pattern. God has established local churches as places of feeding for His people. We are not to float aimlessly from church to church.

I regularly receive letters and calls from people who say they have prophetic ministries. Many claim they don't attend a local church, and I let them know they are out of order! The Scripture says that God sets the prophets in the Church (1 Corinthians 12:28) to perfect the Church. This is another example of the pattern of God being violated to suit our own purposes.

THE PRIORITY OF PRAISE

Orthodox Jews often walk in great revelation concerning God and the things of God, but are blinded to the reality of Christ. They may even speak about Jesus without realizing that they are speaking about Him. One Jewish person stated: "The prayer of praise is always superior to the prayer of petition."

Many Christians do not have that man's wisdom concerning prayer. For instance, some churches discourage clapping, claiming that it is "an Old Testament practice." They don't realize that the Old Testament is a New Testament book. What book did the Early Church use to establish the correctness of its teachings? Obviously, they used the Scripture available to them, the Old Testament. It's essential to understand that the entire Old Testament, from Genesis to Malachi, was and is for the New Testament Church.

For example, the Psalms teaches us how to worship. When Jesus spoke of the scriptures, He referred to the Law, the Prophets, and the Psalms, identifying the Psalms by name. In the Psalms, there are directions for action. We are told to sing, to dance, and to shout.

DISTRACTIONS TO TRUE PRAISE

In praise and worship, we must watch for distractions. We may be very sincere in what we do, yet be sincerely wrong.
In Luke chapter 10, verses 38-40, we read:

"Now it came to pass, as they went, that he entered into a certain village and a certain woman named Martha received him into her house. And she had a sister called Mary, which also sat at Jesus' feet, and heard his word. But Martha was cumbered about much serving, and came to him, and said, Lord, dost thou not care that my sister hath left me to serve alone? Bid her therefore that she help me."

Like Martha, we can become so busy and occupied with the work of ministry that we miss Jesus. There are churches where some people spend every Sunday in the kitchen cooking and preparing a lunch for after the service. They never attend a Sunday morning worship service.

A prophecy was given to one woman: "You need to cease being a Martha and become a Mary." Some find it hard to sit and be still in God's Presence, yet true worship requires one's full attention.

In verse 40, we see that instead of doing as Martha asked, Jesus took the side of Mary. He said she had chosen "the better part." He wasn't saying there was anything wrong with cleaning the house or fixing a meal, He was simply saying that there is a time for everything. There is a time to put everything else aside and simply worship the Lord. No matter how good or right our pattern and routine may be, it must be put aside or at times totally disregarded in deference to the pattern and purpose of God.

STUDY QUESTIONS CHAPTER 4

1. We're to move only with God's _____ and His_____ .

2. Prayer unctioned by the _____ is a sweet smell in the Father's nostrils.

3. In the Bible, everything is _____ ; however, everything in the Bible is not a statement of _____ .

4. Prayer and _____ create an atmosphere in which God can move.

5. "_____" praise is an abomination in the Father's nostrils.

6. We must guard against too much familiarity with God's _____ .

7. When what we build is not according to the _____ , He won't dwell in it.

8. God has established_____ as places of feeding for His people.

9. The entire _____ , from Genesis to Malachi, was and is for the Church.

10. There is a time to put everything else aside and simply _____ the Lord.

RELATIONSHIP: JACOB, RACHEL, AND LEAH

God wants to bring forth a people who will worship Him in Spirit and in Truth. In Genesis 29, verses 16-20, we read:

"And Laban had two daughters: the name of the elder was Leah, and the name of the younger was Rachel. Leah was tender eyed; but Rachel was beautiful and well favoured. And Jacob loved Rachel; and said, I will serve thee seven years for Rachel thy younger daughter. And Laban said, It is better that I give her to thee, than that I should give her to another man: abide with me. And Jacob served seven years for Rachel; and they seemed unto him but a few days, for the love he had to her."

Jacob served Laban because he wanted Rachel as his wife. Notice that Rachel's sister Leah is described as "tender eyed," which means that she had some type of problem with her eyes which affected her appearance.

Verse 21 reads: *"And Jacob said unto Laban, Give me my wife, for my days are fulfilled, that I may go in unto her."* And Laban gathered together all the men of the place, and made a feast. (Genesis 29:22-23)

In ancient Israel, it was customary to have a large feast before a marriage. Sometimes the festivities went on for a week before the actual marriage. Jacob had worked long, hard hours for seven years to have Rachel as his wife. She was his whole goal and focus for seven difficult and trying years.

The story continues, telling how Laban then brought Leah, not Rachel, to Jacob on his wedding night.

In Genesis 29:24-31, we read:

> *"And Laban gave unto his daughter Leah Zilpah his maid for an handmaid.*
> *And it came to pass, that in the morning, behold, it was Leah: and he said to Laban, What is this thou hast done unto me? Did not I serve with thee for Rachel? Wherefore then hast thou beguiled me? And Laban said, It must not be so done in our country, to give the younger before the firstborn. Fulfill her week, and we will give thee this also for the service which thou shalt serve with me yet seven other years. And Jacob did so, and fulfilled her week: and he gave him Rachel his daughter to wife also. And Laban gave to Rachel his daughter Bilhah his handmaid to be her maid. And he went in also unto Rachel, and he loved also Rachel more than Leah, and served with him yet seven other years. And when the Lord saw that Leah was hated, he opened her womb: but Rachel was barren."*

Imagine how Jacob felt when he awoke the morning after his wedding and found that he was with Leah and not Rachel. She was someone for which he had not asked, and not the one for which he had worked so hard.

Leah was in a very bad position. She was an unwanted wife. No doubt, she was hated not only by Jacob, but also by Rachel. There must have been great animosity in the camp. Yet, God allowed Rachel's womb to remain barren. He opened the womb of Leah so that she could be favored. In Old Testament times, it was considered a curse for a woman to be barren. To be fruitful was a sign of blessing.

In Genesis 29:32-33, we read:

> *"And Leah conceived, and bare a son, and she called his name Reuben: for she said, Surely the LORD hath looked upon my affliction; now therefore my husband will love me. And she conceived again, and bare a son; and said, because the Lord hath heard that I was hated, he hath therefore given me this son also: and she called his name Simeon."*

First she had Reuben, a name meaning "behold a son." Then she had Simeon, which means "hearing or to hear." Then in verse 34, we read:

> *"And she conceived again, and bare a son, and said, now this time will my husband be joined unto me, because I have born him three sons: therefore was his name called Levi."*

She was still asking for a relationship with her husband. In verse 35, which is a key verse, we read:

> *"And she conceived again, and bare a son: and she said, Now will I praise the Lord: therefore she called his name Judah; and left bearing."*

The fourth son's name was Judah, which means "praise." In naming him, she was saying, "I shall praise" or "Let me praise," recognizing that God had placed honor upon her. Genesis 30 opens with Rachel's reaction to what was happening:

> *"And when Rachel saw that she bare Jacob no children, Rachel envied her sister; and said unto Jacob, Give me children, or else I die."*

CHILDREN ARE OUR FRUIT

The heart cry of every intercessor, every believer, and every Spirit-filled Christian should be "Lord, give me children, or else I will die!" We are to see children born into the Kingdom of God; to see souls coming into the Kingdom.

Though hated and rejected on every side, Leah gave birth to Judah. It does not matter how much we are hated, or how many times others turn their backs on us; we are to keep praising God. Praise is to come out of our innermost beings.

A PRINCIPLE OF BIBLICAL INTERPRETATION

She called his name "Judah" [Praise]. This is the first mention of praise in the Scriptures. There is a widely accepted, though unwritten law, concerning biblical interpretation. The first mention of anything is to be regarded as very significant. We are to look carefully at exactly how that thing is introduced. In the mind of God, all subsequent mentioning of that thing are somehow connected with the first time it was mentioned.

The first person to use the word "praise" is not someone who has everything she wants, nor someone who is content with her lot in life. Praise (Judah) comes forth from the hated woman. Even when we're hated and things are going against us, we are to praise the Lord God. We are not to complain because complaining rejects the providence of God and renders praise to satan. The meditation of our hearts can become centered on the works of satan, and produce the bitter fruit of frustration, discontentment and rebellion.

A DEFINITION OF PRAISE

The word "praise" comes from the Latin word "pretium" which means "price or value, an inscription of value or worth." Thus, praise means putting value or worth upon something. As I praise God, I'm expressing what God means to me. True over-comers are those who praise God without ceasing, placing all value, worth and honor upon Him.

WHAT IS WORTHY OF PRAISE?

Like many who have travelled in the mission field, I have noticed that poor people often have a very special way of praising God. They know what it means to trust God for the next meal on their table. God wants our praise in the midst of our tight and difficult situations. We are not going to come out of those situations until we learn to praise.

Do you realize some people praise their cars? They send hours cleaning, washing and waxing their cars. Others praise their children. Every other word exalts the accomplishments and activities of their favored offsprings. That kind of praise is good to a point, but when it exceeds the praise of God, there is a problem. Praise can definitely go towards unworthy objects. It can stem from improper motives.

True praise is the sincere acknowledgement of worth, based upon one's real conviction. It expresses how we really feel on the inside towards our Lord and Savior.

Walk through your home praying in the Spirit and praising God. After awhile, you will begin to feel the power of God moving in your being. God will then give purpose and direction to your praise. He will show you things for which you can praise Him. If you have very little in your home, praise God anyway, just for Who He is. We need to be as the three young Hebrew men who praised God in the midst of the fiery furnace. (*See Daniel chapter 3.*)

Sometimes the Lord may have us in a deep place. If we're not careful, the enemy will show us ten thousand reasons why something cannot and will not work out. You and I must stand in the face of that and say, "Lord, I will yet praise You. Lord, I don't care if I'm somehow called to lose all or to be stripped of everything. I don't mind, for I am your vessel. I know that you have the day of elevation coming."

Some of us will be tested to see if we can be stripped of all. Sadly, some of those tested will be as the rich young ruler who said, "I don't want to part with my goods." We may as well let go of our things for the glory of God, for we will lose them anyway. What can we take with us when we leave this world? He that seeks to save his life shall lose it; but the one who seeks to lose it shall save it.

IMPARTATION

In Genesis chapter 49, verses 1 and 2, we see that Jacob was on his deathbed and gathered his sons together.

"And Jacob called unto his sons, and said, Gather yourselves together, that I may tell you that which shall befall you in the last days. Gather yourselves together, and hear, ye sons of Jacob; and hearken unto Israel your father."

He gathered his children around him in order to prophesy over them. I believe that all fathers should go home to the Lord in this way, having expressed the mind of the Lord concerning their children.

We cannot carry over anointings and knowledge which are meant for the earth realm. These need to be imparted so that they can remain. Jesus said, "...the works that I do shall he do also; and greater works than these shall he do ..." (John 14:12). Often a student's achievements will exceed those of his teacher. Once he has learned his lesson, the student then adds what he has been given of his own and takes things further along. When there is an impartation in the Spirit realm, each generation becomes wiser and moves higher in the strength and peace of God.

STUDY QUESTIONS CHAPTER 5

1.   God wants to bring forth a people who will worship Him in _____ .

2.   Praise is to come from our _____ .

3.   _____ is the first person to use the word "praise" (Judah) in the Scriptures.

4.   _____ rejects the providence of God and renders praise to satan.

5.   _____ is the sincere acknowledgement of worth, based upon

one's real conviction.

CHAPTER 6

PRAISE - GOD'S MEANS FOR DELIVERANCE

In Genesis chapter 49, verse 8, we read:

> *"Judah, thou art he whom thy brethren shall praise: thy hand shall be in the neck of thine enemies; thy father's children shall bow down before thee."*

When we praise the Lord, our hand is on the neck of our enemy. The law is reciprocal. In the same way that praise will still the hand of the enemy, the lack of praise will still the Hand of God. God moves on the wings of praise. That's why we read in Psalms 22:3 that He is enthroned upon the praises of Israel.

If we regard it as normal to heap praise upon football heroes and other celebrities, why do we consider it abnormal or strange to praise God with loud voices and demonstrations of our love for Him? How much more should we be giving praise to the King of kings and Lord of lords! We should praise Him exuberantly and without shame, giving Him glory and honor.

The enemy fights a praising people and tries to make them look inferior and silly. He knows that every time we enter into praise, our hands go deeper into his throat. The neck is one of the weakest parts of the human body. Most of the body's nerves are centered in the neck area. A sharp blow to a certain area of the neck can cause paralysis or death. If we praise properly, we are paralyzing the very nerve center of our enemy. Praise stills the enemy.

PREYING ON THE FLESH OF OUR ENEMY

In Genesis chapter 49, verse 9, we read:

"Judah is a lion's whelp: from the prey, my son, thou art gone up: he stooped down, he couched as a lion, and as an old lion; who shall rouse him up?"

Jesus is the Lion of Judah. Lions are associated with boldness and are carnivorous or flesh eating animals. When they catch their prey, they tear away at the animal's flesh. Think about what this Scripture is saying. Whatever fleshly things the enemy sets before us can be torn away through our praise. We can literally feed off the flesh of those things. Our circumstances can be food for our growth. The very thing which the enemy designed to destroy us can be the very thing which will raise us up.

Lions are ferocious animals who move about stealthily or in secret. Often a lion will operate covertly, stalking its prey before making its attack. As we praise, we are able to observe our situation from the position of worship before making our attack to tear away at the very thing designed to destroy us. In launching our attack, we need to praise God for Who He is. Our prayer might be: "Lord, I thank You and praise You that You know all things. You even know the circumstance that I am in and that I can hardly bear it. Lord, I realize You created me and knew me before I came from my mother's womb. I know You will not allow anything to crush me, for I have chosen to establish myself upon the Rock, which is Christ Jesus."

"Lord, I know that You are Omnipotent. All power has been given unto You in heaven and upon earth. I know that You are more powerful than the enemy."

Some people make the mistake of viewing God and satan as equal adversaries on opposing sides. Perhaps you've even seen drawings depicting God and satan having a tug-of-war. This is an erroneous picture! Satan is no match for God! If God says to the devil: "Go," he has to go!

LUCIFER: THE FALLEN ANGEL

Before his fall, satan was called "Lucifer," which means "light bearer." He was created as a beautiful being. In Isaiah 14, verse 11, we read of the judgment which is coming to him; his beauty is going down into the grave.

"Thy pomp is brought down to the grave, and the noise of thy viols: the worm is spread under thee, and the worms cover thee."

Lucifer was once known as the anointed cherub. He is not anointed anymore. He doesn't have the ability to see into things; he only knows what we tell him. He doesn't even know his own, for he said to the seven sons of Sceva, "... Jesus I know, and Paul I know; but who are ye?" (Acts 19:15). He didn't realize Job was in his hands until God told him to open his eyes and see Job right there.

Many people believe that the devil has more strength than he actually has. Yet, the Bible says he is "under our feet." That means we can walk upon him.

When we read about "the noise of thy viols" in Isaiah, it's helpful to realize that a viol is a bow stringed instrument, possibly having six strings. Notice that when satan is buried, so is his musical instrument. Lucifer was a walking instrument. Instruments were created within his very being.

The worms in that passage indicate the presence of decaying organic matter. Worms eat away and strip things of their form and glory. Lucifer was brought down and covered with worms which stripped him of his original glory.

In Ezekiel 28, verse 12, we read again about how Lucifer was created in beauty. Lucifer is a Latin name. His Hebrew name is Halel, from which we get the word "Hallelujah."

"Son of man, take up a lamentation upon the king of Tyrus, and say unto him, Thus saith the Lord GOD; Thou sealest up the sum, full of wisdom, and perfect in beauty."

This is a lamentation against Lucifer. The words "sealest the sum" means, "thou art the finished pattern." Lucifer was created as the finished pattern of praise to God.

Ezekiel chapter 28, verse 13-14 continues, making reference to Lucifer's being in Eden before the creation of Adam:

"Thou hast been in Eden the garden of God; every precious stone was thy covering, the sardius, topaz, and the diamond, the beryl, the onyx, and the jasper, the sapphire, the emerald, and the carbuncle, and gold: the workmanship of thy tabrets and of thy pipes was prepared in thee and of thy pipes was prepared in thee in the day that thou wast created. Thou art the anointed cherub covereth; and I have set thee so: thou wast upon the holy mountain of God; thou hast walked up and down the midst of the stones of fire."

Lucifer was created in great wealth and covered in precious stones. In him were percussion instruments (tabrets), wind instruments (pipes), and, of course, the viols. He was a complete orchestra.

PRAISE: A COVERING FOR THE THRONE OF GOD

It seems possible that Lucifer, the "Cherub that covereth," was created to cover the throne of God with praise. When he fell, God made us to be worshippers, for we are taking the place of Lucifer.

No longer does Lucifer cover the throne with praise. Now we, the believers, do this. When we do not praise God, we leave the throne of God uncovered. That's why Paul says we are to come boldly to the throne of God, for we are to cover His throne with praise.

When an individual, particularly a man, has a problem in praising God, I believe he will have many problems, including pleasing his mate, because he has not allowed his emotions to be released and expressed. If one cannot be free before his Creator, he will not be able to be free before his mate. God deals with the whole man.

THE KEY TO IT ALL IS PRAISE.

In Revelation chapter 4, verses 10-11, we read:

"The four and twenty elders fall down before him that sat on the throne, and worship him that liveth for ever and ever, and cast their crowns before the throne, saying, Thou art worthy, O Lord, to receive glory and honor and power: for thou hast created all things, and for thy pleasure they are and were created."

Each of us was created for the pleasure of God; that is to give praise unto the Lord. We may not feel like praising, especially when we are awakened by the Lord at 4:00 A.M. and told to praise Him. When God nudges us to praise Him, He wants us to cover His throne.

When we go into God's glory, it should be said that the Body of Christ knows how to cover the throne of the Lord, never leaving it exposed. We want it said that the fallen angel was never able to keep the Church from praise.

When we praise, satan becomes jealous and envious, for he is reminded from whence he fell. He is stilled by praise. What shall happens when we praise?

In II Corinthians chapter 3, verses 16 to 18, we read:

"Nevertheless when it shall turn to the Lord, the vail shall be taken away.
Now the Lord is that Spirit: and where the Spirit of the Lord is, there is liberty.
But we all, with open face beholding as in a glass the glory of the Lord, are changed into the same image from glory to glory, even as by the Spirit of the Lord."

As we praise God, we are before His throne with an unveiled face. As we praise Him, we are being changed into His image, going from glory to glory. We become what we praise. If we praise satan, we become like him. If we praise God, we are changed into His image.

STUDY QUESTIONS CHAPTER 6

1. When we praise the Lord, our hand is in the _____ of the enemy.

2. The enemy fights a praising people and tries to make them look _____ and _____.

3. _____ stills the enemy.

4. The very thing by which the enemy designed to _____ us can be the very thing which will _____ us up.

5. We need to praise God for _____ He is and for His _____ .

6. Some people make the mistake of viewing God and satan as _____ adversaries on opposing sides.

7. Lucifer was once known as the _____ cherub.

8. A _____ is a bow stripped instrument, possibly having six strings.

9. He (Lucifer) was a complete _____ . When he fell, God made us to be _____ , for we are taking the place of Lucifer.

CHAPTER 7

LUCIFER AND MUSIC

In Isaiah chapter 14, verses 12-15, we read:

> *"How art thou fallen from heaven, O Lucifer, son of the morning! how art thou cut down to the ground, which didst weaken the nations! For thou hast said in thine heart, I will ascend into heaven, I will exalt my throne above the stars of God: I will sit also upon the mount of the congregation, in the sides of the north: I will ascend above the heights of the clouds; I will be like the most High. Yet thou shalt be brought down to hell, to the sides of the pit."*

The Hebrew word for Lucifer is Halel, from which we derive the word "Hallelujah." Satan's name was "morning star, brightness, or light bearer." The reason he despises us is because he is no longer the light bearer.

Jesus is the light of the world (St. John chapter 8, verse 12). Scripture also says that we are "the light of the world" and "a city set upon a hill" (Matthew chapter 5, verse 14). Note that this "city" is well lit and highly visible. It is not a place, but a people. Every time satan sees us, he is reminded of the place from whence he fell.

Before his fall, satan (who was the morning star) rose before the sun. He swam in the morning light as if that was the source of his birth. Scripture refers to him as the "son of the morning" or "son of the dawn." Isn't it possible that Lucifer's purpose was to bear witness of the light of God, Who is Light?

When we read in Genesis 1:3 that God said, "Let there be light," He was not referring to the sun, moon and stars. All of that was created on the fourth day. Rather, He was saying, "Let God once again appear on the earth."

LUCIFER: "THE SON OF THE MORNING"

Lucifer, which means "light bearer," was also called "the son of the morning." This indicates that God has established from the foundation of the earth that praise will be the beginning of any circumstance or any situation. Because He was the praising angel, Lucifer was the one who started the day.

In the design of the tabernacle, God placed the tents of Judah and Issachar on the side of the east gate, the gate which faced the rising sun. Each day was to begin with praise and worship.

Proverbs 8:17 states, "those that seek me early shall find me." It's important for those who are young to remember their Creator in the days of their youth. The pattern, as revealed in Scripture, is clear. God wants a people who will meet their circumstances early by praising Him.

LUCIFER: "A MUSICAL INSTRUMENT"

Music was originally created for the purposes of God. Thus, it must be fully returned to the church. It's precisely because of its importance to God, that music and the music industry has become so corrupt.

Dance, which will be discussed later in some detail, must also be reintroduced in the church. Not wild, formless dancing, but dance with a pattern. If something lacks a pattern, God is not in the midst of it.

In Ezekiel chapter 28, verses 11-12, we read:

"Moreover the word of the LORD came unto me, saying,
Son of man, take up a lamentation upon the king of Tyrus, and say unto him, Thus saith
the Lord GOD; Thou sealest up the sum, full of wisdom, and perfect in beauty."

Before his fall, Lucifer had the total pattern of God. He understood pattern. When God spoke to Moses about making things for His temple, He said: "Make them after the pattern, which was shewed thee .." (Exodus 25:40). God is a God of structure. If we do not do things according to His pattern, He simply will not live in the midst of what we do.

Lucifer was the finished pattern and the consummation of all beauty and wisdom. God is a God of beauty. (Some people may have come from churches where they were taught that it was wrong to wear gold or jewelry - based upon 1 Timothy 2:9. That's an incorrect interpretation of that Scripture. Paul was saying that we need to put the emphasis on the inward person. It is a quiet spirit which is worth a great price in the eyes of God.)

God loves beauty. He wants His people to have gold, for gold was created by Him. Some "religious people" think that money is evil and dirty, yet money was not created by satan. Actually, money is something godly. We need to develop a respect for it. It is God's will that we prosper and demonstrate His Kingdom in the earth.

LUCIFER - A LESSON IN AVOIDING PRIDE

We read in Ezekiel chapter 28, verse 12 that Lucifer "sealest up the sum, full of wisdom and perfect in beauty." "Sealest" means "to close up or make an end; to mark or set a seal upon." According to Scripture, Lucifer had everything sealed within him.

Having a lot of knowledge can lead to pride. As we become more knowledgeable of the things of God, we need to stoop lower and lower. I once heard wise advice from a respected minister. He said that after preaching a mighty sermon or ministering in a powerful miracle service, one should quickly search out a toilet bowl and begin to clean it. This is to remind ourselves that we are still nothing. It is only in God's power and strength that we act and accomplish. If we want to sit on the throne, we must be willing to clean it. The way up is the way down. That is a Kingdom principle.

In Ezekiel chapter 28, verse 13, we read:

"Thou hast been in Eden the garden of God; every precious stone was thy covering, the sardius, topaz, and the diamond, the beryl, the onyx, and the jasper, the sapphire, the emerald, and the carbuncle, and gold: the workmanship of thy tabrets and of thy pipes was prepared in thee in the day that thou wast created."

Here, Ezekiel talks about the workmanship of the tabrets and the pipes. Workmanship has to do with service. They were expressions of God and vehicles that God used to speak forth His Word. When played under the anointing of God, a musical instrument can begin to prophesy (instruments can speak.) As Lucifer played his instruments, they were speaking as the oracles of God throughout the universe.

This Scripture clearly tells us that Lucifer held money, wealth, riches, music, and the arts. These are now being restored within the churches. The Lord is going to take today's wandering minstrels and snatch the wandering out of them. They will be turned back to the house of God. Musicians aren't going to go from church to church playing to entertain and perform. They will be set as stones within the temple.

Music and prophecy must work hand in hand. A prophet cannot move forward in the degrees of God until he is covenantly married to a minstrel. Music is essential to experience a strong prophetic flow. The musicians will begin to play and pull the Word of the Lord from the mouths of the prophets, and they will prophesy in the Spirit of the Living God.

COVERING THE THRONE OF GOD
Ezekiel chapter 28, verse 14, reads:
> *"Thou art the anointed cherub that covereth; and I have set thee so: thou wast upon the holy mountain of God; thou hast walked up and down in the midst of the stones of fire."*

Lucifer was quite possibly created to cover God's throne. Satan understands the idea of covering, no doubt much more than most Christians do. People who are without a church and a shepherd, who say, "Jesus is my teacher," are in danger. They are uncovered. When it begins to rain there is nothing to shield them from the elements. There is no covering and no relating to God's purposes.

Isn't it possible that now we are being raised up to cover the very throne of God with our praise and that we are God's covering? The model prayer of Jesus begins not with begging, but with praising. We must first enter into His Presence and into His courts with praise.

BEING UNDER AUTHORITY - GOD'S QUALIFICATION
In 1 Samuel chapter 10, Samuel took a vial of oil to anoint a king. Saul was looking for the asses which belonged to his father, Kish (see chapter 9). Possibly Saul was qualified to be king at that time because he was under authority. He was out doing the bidding of his father.

Before someone can be a man or woman of authority, they must be a man or woman under authority. We need to strongly avoid those not under authority. When people claim that they are operating in the Holy Ghost, yet say that they don't have control over what they say or do, they are wrong. They are not under the anointing of the Holy Ghost. The spirit of the prophet is subject to the prophet. If a spirit has a person so out of himself that he is unaware of his environment, or feels that he is out of control, there is something wrong with that spirit. The Holy Ghost will not cause a person to go crazy.

After Samuel anointed Saul to be "captain over his inheritance," he told Saul where to find the asses he was looking for. He then told him to go forward to the plain of Tabor.

In 1 Samuel 10, verse 5, we read:

> *"After that thou shalt come to the hill of God, where is the garrison of the Philistines: and it shall come to pass, when thou art come thither to the city, that thou shalt meet a company of prophets coming down from the high place with a psaltery, and a tabret, and a pipe, and a harp, before them; and they shall prophesy:"*

Notice, Saul did not meet just one prophet, but he met a company of prophets. The Lord is saying that in this day, men and women will minister in companies rather than as soloists. In a company, a person has to flow, knowing his or her part and understanding their boundaries.

MINOR PROPHETS

God is going to bring together major and minor prophets. The word "minor" refers to the depth or degree with which God will use a person in ministry.

God has governmental gifts in the "Body." We must be watchful in getting a word from a "minor" prophet as the word may or may not be accurate. It is easier to go off key when singing in a minor key than when singing in a major key. The "major" prophet, therefore, needs to take the lead role.

THE SCHOOL OF THE PROPHETS

1 Samuel chapter 10 refers to a "company of prophets" or a "school of prophets." The group was also known as "sons of the prophets." Samuel was the first one to establish a "school of prophets" and he used music to train up young prophets.

In order for someone to be in a school of prophets, he had to look to his teacher as his father. When Elisha saw Elijah get caught up, he cried out: "My father, my father ..." There cannot be a degree of impartation or of life until the student can recognize the teacher as father. In the New Testament, Paul refers to "My son, Timothy."

Many will come to a school to learn and will get something. However, there are those who will cling and say, "Father, this is the one You have placed me under. I will look to him as a father in the Gospel." There will then be a greater degree of impartation and life.

In the school of prophets, they were trained in poetry, history and music. Poetry and history taught them structure and pattern. A knowledge of a people's past tells where they are going. If we look at someone's past, we can almost determine their destiny.

History can intimidate some. They will refer to it and say, "We cannot do this." or "This was never done before." Or they will say, "When this was done in the past, it caused so much confusion and people were moved off base." History and statistics need not be intimidating. Once God has spoken something, He will back up His Word and bring that thing to pass.

MUSIC AND PROPHECY

Music is vital in the school of prophets. In learning music, we learn timing, rhythm and harmony. Some prophets are out of harmony and always in the wrong key, not understanding the difference between time and the fullness of time. We need to wait until a word matures and God begins to release it. When we move in the right timing, rhythm and harmony, God conveys a beautiful message to His people.

I believe, as many other writers, David spent much time in or around the school of prophets. This may explain why he was so in tune with the worship of God and was able to build a tabernacle. Running from Saul, we know that he hid among the prophets. There was safety among the prophets, for in that place there was direction. When we are in trouble, the place to hide is among the prophets.

1 Samuel tells us that the prophets came with a psaltery. The Hebrew word for "psaltery" is "nebel." It refers to a 10-string harp. The strings are stretched in a triangle form with the longest string forming the base. The tabret (in Hebrew toph) is a tambourine struck by hand. The pipe (in Hebrew chalil) is a kind of flute. It's quite possible that David learned to prophesy upon the instruments in the school of the prophets.

Notice that the instruments mentioned in 1 Samuel are the same ones Ezekiel describes as being part of Lucifer.

These instruments seem to be related to the prophets of God or those who speak as the oracles of God. There is a definite relationship between music, instruments and prophecy.

Music stirs the soul of the prophet. In 2 Kings chapter 3, the king of Israel, the king of Edom, and Jehoshaphat went to see the prophet Elisha. Elisha was troubled by their coming and asked them why they had not sought prophets from among their own people. They told him that they needed to come to him because they needed to hear the Word of the Lord.

There are times when this can trouble the soul of the prophet. For instance, once I had some leaders come to me who said they wanted to hear the Word of the Lord. I felt troubled. They prayed and then were waiting for me to prophesy. I felt disturbed and sensed that they had done some wrong things. They said, "Do you have a word for us?" I told them, "No." They said, "That's strange. You usually have a Word of the Lord, and we know you are a prophet."

I told them that I simply did not have anything to say to them. After they left, someone asked me why I had not prophesied. I told him that I had been disturbed in my spirit and that I had felt the need for a minstrel.

In II Kings, we read how Elisha was troubled, and he said, "Now bring me a minstrel." He needed the music to quiet his soul so that the Spirit of God could seep through and give him the Word of the Lord.

Clearly there is a relationship between the ministry of the prophet and the minstrel. When Elisha called for the minstrel, "... The hand of the Lord came upon him (II Kings 3:15). Whenever music goes forth, God's Hand begins to rest upon the people and the soul of the prophet is stirred.

The Hebrew word for "minstrel" is "nagan," which means "harper." A minstrel is one who "beats a tune with their fingers, playing upon a stringed instrument."

Psalms 144, verse 1, reads:
> *"Blessed be the LORD my strength, which teacheth my hands to war, and my fingers to fight:"*

Those who are playing instruments in worship are using their fingers to fight. They are in spiritual warfare.

Psalms 22, verse 3, reads:
> *"But thou art holy, O thou that inhabitest the praises of Israel."*

To "inhabit" means "to make a sanctuary." When the Lord inhabits the praise of Israel, he makes a sanctuary upon the praises of His people. The Hebrew word for "inhabitest" is "yashab" which means "to sit down, as a judge in ambush; to dwell or remain; to settle or to be married." Another translation of Psalms 22 is, "He is enthroned upon the praises of Israel." Jesus comes down as judge and sets ambushment and works with circumstances. The King of Glory actually comes down and judges circumstances.

Can you see the value of beginning your day with praise? When we do this, we begin the day by unseating the devil and by letting God be seated upon the throne.

Revelation 2:13 speaks of "satan's seat" being in the church in Pergamos. A church that moves into worshipping God in Spirit and in Truth will unseat satan and cause God to be seated in that House instead. Now you know why the enemy has such hatred of praise and worship.

STUDY QUESTIONS - CHAPTER 7

1. Every time satan sees _____, he is reminded of the place from which he fell.

2. God wants a people who will meet their _____ early by praising Him.

3. _____ was originally created for the purposes of God.

4. When played under the anointing of God, an _____ can begin to prophesy.

5. Before someone can be a man or woman _____ authority, they must be a man or woman _____ authority.

6. _____ was the first one to establish a school of the prophets, and he used music to train up young prophets.

7. Music was and is vital in the _____ .

8. The _____ is a 10-string harp; the _____ is a tambourine; and the _____ is a kind of flute.

9. There seems to be a relationship between music, instruments, _____ and _____.

10. A _____ is one who "beats a tune with their fingers,_____ playing upon a stringed instrument.

11. When the Lord inhabits the praise of Israel, he makes a _____ upon the praises of His people.

12. A church that moves into worshipping God in spirit and truth _____ will _____ satan.

CHAPTER 8

A DEFINITION OF MUSIC

Webster's dictionary defines music as "the art or science of harmonic sounds." The first place music is mentioned in the Bible is in Genesis, which is a book of beginnings. The seed of almost every truth is found in this book.

The etymology or root meaning of a word often provides important clues to its meaning. This is also true when referring to the names of individuals in the Scriptures. For instance, the name Isaac means "laughter." When his mother Sarah, who was very elderly, heard the prophetic word that she would become a mother, she laughed. Could it be that she was healed and made able to conceive at that time? The Bible does say that "a merry heart is like a medicine."

Let's look at Genesis, chapter 4, verse 20, and consider the meaning of one of the names there.

> "And Adah bare Jabal: he was the father of such as dwell in tents, and of such as have cattle. And his brother's name was Jubal: he was the father of all such as handle the harp and organ."

The name "Jubal" means "a player on an instrument," or "a musician." Jubal played the harp (in Hebrew "kinnor") which was a stringed instrument. From this Scripture, we know that even from the earliest times, man created and had access to musical instruments. Jubal also played the organ (coming from the root word meaning "to breathe or to blow). Generally it refers to a wind instrument, something like a shepherd's reed or flute.

Jubal's brother was Jabal, whose name means "a traveler or producer." The name comes from the Hebrew word "Yabal" which means "to flow or be poetic." This Scripture tells us that the arts were being formed out of the lineage of Cain. Music was created on one hand and poetry or flowing rhythm was created on the other.

ANOINTED MUSIC

Anointed music not only soothes the soul, but it also has the ability to bring or draw out the Word of the Lord. That's why it's so important to enter into praise and worship. Worship is essential to a church service. It has been noted that in every move of God, there is something that God magnifies. Whatever is magnified becomes central to church services. In 1906 there was a move around tongues. Things centered around tongues and whether or not people had received the gift of tongues. In the healing revival, things centered around the healing service. In the 1970's, the word movement brought focus on the preaching of the Word.

Now we are in a new movement. The next move is coming on the wings of worship and the wings of praise. Praise and worship are becoming the center, with everything else revolving around these two things. God is raising up a people who will worship and praise Him.

The praise and worship will be so intense that some will think the participants are crazy. We need not fear their judgments, for some will be drawn to services to see the "crazy people" and leave as believers. God will use even the misguided things people say about His children to accomplish His purposes.

THE ROLE OF THE MINSTREL

In II Kings chapter 3, starting at verse 12, we read:

> "And Jehoshaphat said, The word of the Lord is with him. So the king of Israel and Jehoshaphat and the king of Edom went down to him. And Elisha said unto the king of Israel, What have I to do with thee? Get thee to the prophets of thy father, and to the prophets of thy mother. And the king of Israel said unto him, Nay: for the Lord hath called these three kings together, to deliver them into the hand of Moab. And Elisha said, As the Lord of hosts liveth, before whom I stand, surely, were it not that I regard the presence of Jehoshaphat the king of Judah, I would look toward thee, nor see thee."

First, notice Elisha began to rebuke Jehoshaphat in verse 13, asking him why he hadn't gone to the prophets of his mother and father. In other words, "Go somewhere else. You've been serving and listening to someone else. Why now, when you are in deep trouble, are you seeking out the man of God?" I can relate to this personally because I get calls asking for the Word of the Lord from people who come around only when they are in deep trouble and distress.

Second, we see in verse 14 that Elisha understood that his primary responsibility was to God. He didn't get thrown off course because he was standing in the presence of great men.

You may recall the account about Naaman, the captain of the Syrian army, who was a leper. The prophet Elisha told him to go wash in the Jordan River seven times and that afterwards, he would be cleansed. Naaman went away enraged at what the prophet said. To him, the Jordan was a dirty, muddy river in a foreign land. The prophet didn't regard the rank of the man in front of him or Naaman's reaction. Rather, he honored God first. Elisha told Naaman what God said.

In II Kings 3:15, Elisha requests that a minstrel be brought to him. The Hand of the Lord came upon him, and he spoke, "For thus saith the Lord, make this valley full of ditches."

MUSIC FOR WARFARE

Music is inspirational and can influence work and warfare. When Jehoshaphat wanted to wage war, he sent for a minstrel who could create an atmosphere for God to dwell in.

King Saul used music to soothe his troubled spirit. When the evil spirits came to torment him, he had David play upon the harp.

Playing the harp saved David's life many times. David had many revelations about music. He knew that praise had literally saved his life. He understood firsthand that praise could soothe and curtail the attack of his enemy.

When in deep trouble, a wise person seeks out a prophet, someone with the Word of the Lord. The prophetic Word of the Lord can save lives. I have witnessed this. People were headed towards total destruction. They heard the Word of the Lord and their lives were totally changed. The Word of the Lord is valuable and needs to be treasured.

Several scriptures specifically record how, after music was played, the word of the Lord was brought forth. One place, as mentioned earlier in this book, is Psalms 22: "My God, my God, why hast thou forsaken me? Why art thou so far from helping me ..."

It is verse 3 of this Psalm which is the key here. In it, the psalmist recognizes that although it may appear as though God has forsaken us, he has not. "But thou art holy, O thou that inhabitest the praises of Israel." He dwells within praise. Jesus Christ is there, in the midst of our praise, judging situations. Our praise creates an atmosphere for the Father to set up His throne. As we continue our praise and our confession of faith, we will see His will unfold before us.

STUDY QUESTIONS CHAPTER 8

1. Webster's dictionary defines _____ as "the art or science of harmonic sounds."

2. The etymology or _____ of a word often provides important clues to its meaning.

3. Even from the earliest times man created and had access to_____ .

4. The _____ were formed out of the lineage of Cain.

5. Anointed music not only soothes, it also has the ability to _____ bring or draw out the _____ of the _____ .

6. The next move (of God) is coming on the wings of _____ and the wings of _____ .

7. Music is for work and for _____ .

8. David understood firsthand that praise could soothe and _____ curtail the _____ of the enemy.

9. When in deep trouble, a wise person seeks out a_____ ; someone with the Word of the Lord.

10. Our praise creates an atmosphere for the Father to set up His _____.

CHAPTER 9

Music will be a part of the occupation of those in heaven. In Revelation 5, verse 9, we read about the "new song" being sung before the Lamb.

"And they sung a new song, saying, Thou are worthy to take the book, and open the seals
thereof: for thou wast slain, and hast redeemed us to God by thy blood out of every kin-
dred, and tongue, and people, and nation."

There will be new songs sung throughout eternity. Life is just a vapor. People leave this earth and go on to another place. Those in ministry need to learn to enter into God's rest. We must understand that our ministry is not to one another, but to the Lord. As we minister to Him, the people will be ministered to. When we lose the Lord as our center of focus, and begin ministering to people, ministry can quickly become a deadly burden.

IN HIS TIME

Do you know that God confessed Jesus for 4,000 years before He actually came upon the earth in the flesh? How many times have we gone into great distress when something we have been confessing hasn't come to pass within a week or two? God lives in an eternal day. He is simply never late. We say, "I must get busy! I have to get going with this project!" Meanwhile, God may be sitting back in heaven saying, "Hold on! Wait a few minutes."

Have you ever observed small children in the shopping mall with parents? Suddenly, they'll decide they want some ice cream, and they begin to tug on their mother's sleeve. "I want some ice cream!" The mother says, "Wait a few minutes. I am looking at this dress." The child impatiently continues tugging and crying.

"No, I want the ice cream now!" Isn't this indicative of our response to God? Do we ever stop to hear the Lord saying, "I will give you the ice cream, but there are other more pressing things to be done right now!"

Sometimes, we resort to giving the Lord an ultimatum. "I'll go on a five day fast. Then Lord, You will surely act!" Our fasting becomes our way of tugging at God's arm to get Him to say, "Yes."

Meanwhile, God is teaching us to wait upon Him. The lesson for the day may well be patience. "Let patience have her perfect work" (James 1:4). "Be careful for nothing" (Philippians 4:6).

IN HIS WAY

The book of Exodus opens with the moaning and groaning of the Israelites who were in slavery under the Egyptians. The word "exodus" means "the way out." The Israelites were looking for a way out of their bondage.

In the first verse of chapter 15, Moses joins with the people in song. Every leader in the church must be a worshipper. In too many churches, during the worship service, the pastor is sitting near the pulpit observing the worship. He may get up for a moment and tell the congregation, "Go ahead children. Praise God today." He then sits down again until it is time for his sermon.

Hopefully, the day of such pastors is ending. The one to give direction to the worship should be the leader. One reason why so many people don't know how to praise God is because their leaders haven't demonstrated how to do it. In fact, the leaders have been sitting down or have been busy with something else during the worship. People can only go as far as the leader takes them.

ACCORDING TO HIS PURPOSES

Having just experienced the glorious things the Lord had done in the lives of His people, Moses led the Israelites in song.

In Exodus chapter 15, verse 1, we read:

> *"Then sang Moses and the children of Israel this song unto the LORD, and spake, saying, I will sing unto the LORD, for he hath triumphed gloriously: the horse and his rider hath he thrown into the sea."*

This is the first time in the Scriptures that we find joint singing. There is a suggestion that Israel had some type of choir. Perhaps they sang as they crossed the Red Sea, for the people quickly responded in song to what had happened. The song of Moses was partially historic and partially prophetic, painting a glorious picture of the future. The song of the Lord will often be that way, embodying the two aspects.

Some of the old gospel songs came out of the days of slavery. Songs such as "Steal Away," "Swing Low, Sweet Chariot" and "sometimes, "I Feel Like a Motherless Child" have emerged from the time when slaves were running from unjust masters searching for their exodus.

When we are born again, though our earthly parents might totally forsake us, we know that we are cared for by the Lord. He is our Mother and our Father. This reality is going to be reflected more and more in our church music. God is going to put a new song in our mouths. We are going to be singing out both our current experiences and that which God is saying prophetically for this day. Songs from the past which do not relate to our current experience will be sung less and less. God wants to take us to a new plateau, putting His song in our mouths and giving His Word to the church.

WOMEN AND PRAISE

In Exodus chapter 15, verse 20, we read:

> *"And Miriam the prophetess, the sister of Aaron, took a timbrel in her hand; and all the women went out after her with timbrels and with dances."*

As Miriam, Moses' sister, began to dance, all of the women joined in with her. We are going to be taught how to flow in the Spirit of the Lord. When one is dancing, we will learn how to join with that person in the dance.

The Israelites had just left the oppression of Egypt. Surely, they hadn't been able to dance in Egypt, nor did they have anything to sing about there. Their harps had been hung on the willow trees.

In chapter 6, verse 4 of Micah, reference is made back to Moses, Aaron and Miriam, who were sent by the Lord before the people of Israel as He led them out of

Egypt. Thus, Miriam is given clear recognition as a leader of Israel. She is referred to as a prophetess in Exodus 15 and stands with her brother Aaron to be punished for going against Moses' marriage in Numbers 12. Women can surely be leaders within the Church of God.

As Miriam led the women in praise, she played the timbrel or tambourine. This instrument originated in Egypt and was generally played by women. There was a separation of women and men in worship, following after an Egyptian custom.
Verse 21 of Exodus 15 tells how the singing and dancing of Miriam and the other women followed upon the song of Moses:

> "And Miriam answered them, Sing ye to the LORD, for he hath triumphed gloriously; the horse and his rider hath he thrown into the sea."

It is as though Miriam led the chorus of women to answer the chorus of men. They were singing back and forth, a song of praise unto the Lord.

CHOOSING MUSICIANS

The musician had an important role in the nation of Israel.
In I Chronicles chapter 15, verses 16-17, we read:

> "And David spake to the chief of the Levites to appoint their brethren to be the singers with instruments of musick, psalteries and harps and cymbals, sounding, by lifting up the voice with joy. So the Levites appointed Heman the son of Joel; and of his brethren, Asaph the son of Berechiah: and of the sons of Merari their brethren, Ethan the son of Kushaiah;"

Musicians were chosen vessels to minister before the Lord. There must be a call upon the life of a musician.

In I Chronicles chapter 6, verses 31-32, we read:

> "And these are they whom David set over the service of song in the house of the LORD, after that the ark had rest. And they ministered before the dwelling place of the tabernacle of the congregation with singing, until Solomon had built the house of the LORD in Jerusalem: and then they waited on their office according to their order."

Here again, the musicians were chosen by David who was the leader. He didn't take the full responsibility for actually getting the musicians, but assigned that task to the Levites or priests who were involved in music.

Musicians, singers and dancers were assigned to accompany the Ark of the Covenant. The Ark denotes the Presence of God. There was an actual procession of singers and musicians going before the Ark as it was carried forth into the Tabernacle. Today, musicians and singers still bring the Presence of God into the sanctuary.

We're approaching the time when musicians and singers will once again usher in the powerful Presence of God, to the point where those ministering will not be able to stand. The worship will have created an atmosphere for the Lord of Hosts to dwell in. The chosen Old Testament musicians played three types of instruments:

1. The Psalter. (This was an oblong box or sounding board with strings. These were the string instruments.)
2. Harps.
3. Cymbals.

According to the Scriptures, the musicians they appointed were also singers. Apparently, they formed three choirs according to which instrument a person played. I've never seen this done in a choir, but it seems that the musicians played and sang at the same time.

STUDY QUESTIONS CHAPTER 9

1. Music will be a part of the _____ of those in heaven.

2. We truly need to understand that our _____ is not to one another but to the Lord.

3. The word_____ means "the way out."

4. One reason why so many people don't know how to praise God is because their _____ haven't told them or showed them how to do it.

5. The song of Moses was partially _____ and partially _____ , painting a glorious picture of the future.

6. _____ can surely be leaders within the Church of God.

7. The timbrel originated in _____ and was generally played by women.

8. There must be a _____ if the Lord upon the life of the musician.

9. _____ and _____ will once again usher in the powerful Presence of God.

10. The _____ musicians played three types of instruments: the psalter, harps and cymbals.

CHAPTER 10

THE PROPHETIC WORD OF THE LORD:

"I am calling thee to create a habitation of worship; to create a habitation of praise. I am going to ride upon the wings of your praise that shall soar to new heights in My Presence. This is the day which shall mark new beginnings for many. For this is the season that I shall move you out of the comfort of the eagle's nest into the realms of My Power and My Glory.

I'm going to begin to do a brand new thing within you. I'm going to break up the fallow ground of your heart that you may become all that I have destined thee to become. That which was spoken of by the prophet Joel, shall become a living reality within you. I shall pour out My Spirit upon all flesh! And yea, your sons and your daughters shall prophesy! I shall cause those that are extremely young to begin to move in the things of the Lord. The Word of the Lord shall begin to come forth even out of the mouth of babes and sucklings. And you shall know that the Hand of the Lord has been stretched towards thee this day. Enter in! Enter in! For as you determine to enter into My Presence and create a habitation, I will dwell in thy midst, and I will continually speak unto thee.

My Spirit is going to begin to move over the nations of this world. I am going to raise up an army of people who are going to create an atmosphere for the enthronement of my presence in their midst.

I am going to begin to shape political powers and political structures. And yea, My Kingdom is going to begin to be established. This is the day whereby My signs and wonders are *going to come forth in great intensity. And yea, My Word shall burn in the mouths of the prophets of the Most High God.*

The day is now approaching when they are going to go to leaders of nations and speak to men in high places, saying Hear ye the Word of the Lord for your land and for your city. I am going to raise up people in despised places and regions and place honor upon them and give them a new degree of My glory.

Begin to arm yourselves, for the day will come when you will join in praise with them, and your eyes shall behold the habitation of the Lord. And I shall begin to topple the altars and high places down of the vain imaginations of men who shall extol Me, and see me for Who I am, saith the Spirit of Almighty God."

THE PROPHETIC SONG

The Holy Spirit has already begun to demonstrate some things about the Song of the Lord in our day.

In II Chronicles chapter 29, verse 27, we read:

> *"And Hezekiah commanded to offer the burnt offering upon the altar. And when the burnt offering began, the song of the LORD began also with the trumpets, and with the instruments ordained by David king of Israel."*

As they placed the burnt offering upon the altar, the Israelites began to praise. Similarly, as we begin to offer up our sacrifice, the Lord wants us to know that it is time for the songs and music to begin. Indeed, our sacrifice is to be a sacrifice of praise. Prophetic songs can also be used as spiritual songs. Thus, they may contain a prophetic Word of the Lord to man, and they may also contain a word of praise to the Lord. Anyone wanting to be a prophet or flow in the prophetic ministry must first learn to sing spiritual songs.

A pastor once taught and shared many wonderful things at one session of the School of the Prophets. One important insight was that if God cannot trust you to sing a song from your heart to Him, He cannot trust you to sing a song from His heart to His people.

In Corinthians 14:15, Paul says:

> *"What is it then? I will pray with the spirit, and I will pray with the understanding also: I will sing with the spirit, and I will sing with the understanding also."*

II Chronicles tells us that the Israelites played trumpets and instruments ordained by King David in their services. Clearly, they had definite order in their worship services. In the Old Testament, they even prophesied according to the order of the king. This order is being reestablished within the church today. People will no longer be able to come into places of worship and just randomly take part.

In I Chronicles 25, verse 7, we read:

"So the number of them, with their brethren that were instructed in the songs of the LORD, even all that were cunning, was two hundred fourscore and eight."

The thing to notice here is that clever, skilled musicians were chosen or picked out by the king and instructed in the songs of the Lord. There was a definite order as to how things were done.

PRAISE: A LIFTING UP

The Hebrew word for song is "massa," which means "prophecy, a burden lifted up or an utterance." In the Old Testament, the burden lifted up was symbolized by the physical lifting up of the Ark of the Covenant. As we bring forth our song, there will be a lifting of our burden and a lifting up of God's Presence in our worship services.

When the Israelites were in the wilderness and the cloud of glory moved, people moved with the cloud. There was no such thing as sitting back and basking in God's Presence. Those who didn't move with the cloud knew that they would be in trouble, for they would be out of the Presence of God, and exposed to the elements.

THE SONG OF THE LORD FOR WAR

The Song of the Lord is beginning to have new meaning and new purpose in the church. In Psalms 22:22 and Hebrews 2:12, we see that Jesus Christ sings in the midst of the church. All singing comes from breath, and Jesus is the Breath of God. Jesus is the Song. He is the theme of the song.

FEAR VERSUS FAITH

In Ephesians chapter 6, verse 12, we read:

"For we wrestle not against flesh and blood, but against principalities, against powers, against the rulers of the darkness of this world, against spiritual wickedness in high places."

We, being the light of the world, come into situations bringing the Lordship of Christ - the Kingdom of God. The altars and high places in our lives that exalt themselves above God have got to come down.

When Israel came out of Egypt, it was difficult to get Egypt out of the people's hearts. Some desired to return. In Exodus chapter 16, we read how they began murmuring against Moses and Aaron. They accused them of bringing them into the wilderness "to kill this whole assembly with hunger" (verse 3).

Later, in chapter 32, we read how they became afraid when Moses was delayed in returning from Mount Sinai. They commanded Aaron to build a golden calf for them to worship. In their fear, they turned totally against God. They literally abandoned the protective Presence of God for the idolatrous presence of a man-made golden calf. This was in spite of all that they had actually seen God do in getting them out of Egypt and across the Red Sea.

Fear brings torment to the spirit, soul, and body. Fear is the opposite of faith. A person who is fearful is not of much use to God.

FEAR VERSUS PRAISE

Webster's dictionary defines fear as "to be alarmed or in apprehension of danger." Some people are alarmists and want to alarm others. "Did you hear the news today?" More to the point, suppose a church is being established in an inner city area. The alarmist will tell you, "You want to visit that church? Do you have any idea what that area is like?"

Are we people of faith or of fear? Is the earth still the Lord's and the fullness thereof? If we believe that the Kingdom is going to come in our lives and dwell in us, fear must be removed. We must rise up as men and women of God, standing in covenant with God. "No weapon that is formed against me shall prosper, and every tongue that rises up in judgment against me I will condemn it." (See Isaiah 54:17.)

In 2 Chronicles 20:2, we read that Jehoshaphat, the king of Judah, heard that a great multitude of soldiers were about to come against him in battle. Verse 3 says, "And Jehoshaphat feared, and set himself to seek the Lord, and proclaimed a fast throughout all Judah." This was the first time a general fast by royal proclamation is recorded in the Scriptures.

In 2 Chronicles 20:6-12, we read how the king invoked a God who had universal authority. The God he invoked is a covenant keeping God and is put in remembrance of His covenant. "Art not thou our God, who didst drive out the inhabitants of this land before thy people Israel, and gavest it to the seed of Abraham thy friend for ever" (verse 7). God is reminded of His promise to Israel.

There is a pattern here for all of us on how to conduct spiritual warfare. When we see that the devil is trying to rob us of the promises of God, God wants us to put Him in remembrance of His Word concerning that thing. God is a covenant keeping God. We truly need to understand the contract. If we lack understanding of the contract, we will not know that we have a right to expect from God what He has promised to us.

In 2 Chronicles chapter 20, verses 14-16, we read:

"Then upon Jahaziel the son of Zechariah, the son of Benaiah, the son of Jeiel, the son of Mattaniah, a Levite of the sons of Asaph, came the Spirit of the LORD in the midst of the congregation. And he said, Hearken ye, all Judah, and ye inhabitants of Jerusalem, and thou king Jehoshaphat, Thus saith the LORD unto you, Be not afraid nor dismayed by reason of this great multitude; for the battle is not yours, but God's. To morrow go ye down against them: behold, they come up by the cliff of Ziz; and ye shall find them at the end of the brook, before the wilderness of Jeruel."

Jahaziel was a priest, a Levite, and a son of Asaph (which means "a gatherer".) Interestingly enough, he was a singer. It seems all the priests were musically incline. And he began to prophesy the Word of the Lord over a heathen nation.

There is a pattern here, for in our day we are going to hear people singing the Song of the Lord over nations, cities, states and countries. In our day as in the day of Jahaziel, this prophetic singing will bring about change.

Jahaziel's word, remember, was coming against a godless nation. God wants us to prophesy to our Goliaths. When Goliath was coming towards David, David prophesied what he was going to do. The giant also prophesied as to what he was going to do to Israel, but David had the sure word of prophecy.

David spoke to the men of Israel around him and said, ".... For who is this uncircumcised Philistine, that he should defy the armies of the living God?" (I Samuel 17:26).

Circumcision was a sign of the covenant. Thus, David was speaking out that Goliath was a man who had no covenant with God. God did not recognize him. How could he dare to defy the army of God? He had no covenant with God.

David understood covenant. He picked up those five smooth stones from the brook where they were lying together. God is bringing people together who will relate to one another. He will gather those who are related and move upon them, and cause them to be thrust forward as five smooth stones to defeat the works of satan. Going back to II Chronicles, we see the importance of releasing the prophetic word against the enemy. After that they positioned themselves for battle. In a battle, it is essential that everyone knows how to be a joint that supplies. (Ephesians 4:16.) In II Chronicles chapter 20, verse 18, we read:

> "And Jehoshaphat bowed his head with his face to the ground: and all Judah and the inhabitants of Jerusalem fell before the LORD, worshipping the LORD."

Here was a situation similar to one we might face at some point in our lives. It was a situation so grave that it called for all the people of a nation to fall upon their faces before God. After Jehoshaphat bowed down in worship, the others around him began to act;

In II Chronicles chapter 20, verse 19, we read:

> "And the Levites, of the children of the Kohathites, and of the children of the Korhites, stood up to praise the LORD God of Israel with a loud voice on high."

Notice that the praise was loud and expressive; it was the kind of praising that many have trouble with today. Yet, we know that such praise is a part of heaven.

When Jehoshaphat bowed, according to the Hebrew meaning of "bowed", he bent his body and stooped with his face to the ground. Remember that worship means "to become prostrate or to fall on one's knees before the Lord with one's forehead touching the ground; as to be prostrate to reverence; like a god kissing its master's hand." Our worship is to be like that, bowing down and kissing the Hand of the Lord. He wants us to stoop low in worship, so that we can give glory unto His Name.

In verse 21 Jehoshaphat begins to gather the people for action.

> "And when he had consulted with the people, he appointed singers unto the LORD, and that should praise the beauty of holiness, as they went out before the army, and to say, Praise the LORD; for his mercy endureth for ever."

Notice, things were done in order. People were appointed to sing. In so many of our churches today, if someone comes to a service who is known to have a good singing voice, they are quickly invited up front to sing. Music is a ministry unto the Lord. It is just as important as the preaching of the Word. The musicians at a service need to be those who have been called and appointed to minister to a particular body at a particular time.

The singers were appointed to praise the Lord in "the beauty of holiness." The beauty of holiness means with garments of beauty, ornaments adorning. When you understand the Hebrew text, you learn that the priests actually went out to war adorned in the latest fashions. All of the arts, even fashion, were created to praise God.

Years ago in churches, those who led worship were often specially dressed. This is something that might properly be restored in the church by having those leading worship wear some kind of formal dress. Certainly, in the Old Testament, worship leaders were beautifully clothed in garments trimmed with gold and precious stones upon their breastplates.

As I studied all this, the Lord impressed upon me that clothing is important. Clothing denotes covering and makes a statement. It is widely recognized that a person's style of dress makes an immediate statement about a person, no matter what the occasion may be. Dress does a certain type of warfare for the person and often sets up a positive first impression, making others receptive to what is to come.

When the priests went forward adorned in fine linens and wearing precious ornaments, they were making a statement to their enemies. They were the conquerors, coming in to take the spoils. Even when a person feels like he or she is losing, they need to look like they are winners. Corporations which are struggling, often make a particular effort to look prosperous. Otherwise, no one would want to invest in them.

Sometimes people don't want to be part of the Kingdom of God because we have made it look like a place of hardship and struggle. Unfortunately, the church has often helped encourage this kind of mentality, by erroneous teaching which equated poverty awareness of attire with holiness.

In 2 Chronicles, chapter 20, verse 22, we read:
"And when they began to sing and to praise, the LORD set ambushments against the children of Ammon, Moab, and mount Seir, which were come against Judah; and they were smitten."

The setting of ambushments meant that the Lord set persons to lie in wait. The Targums is an Aramaic translation of the Old Testament books. In the Hebrew, Targum means "interpretation," indicating the Israelites' ancient belief that angelic powers went into operation when they began to praise God. When we begin to praise the Lord, the angels start to go to work. It may look like nothing is happening, but when we praise

God, angelic powers start to go in and conquer our enemy. Praise is the weapon and instrument of warfare.

AFTER THE BATTLE: PROSPERITY

Some interesting things happened after that battle in Chronicles. The Israelites prospered. After any spiritual battle we fight, we come out with prosperity. Those who are fighting constant battles, who see little prosperity, might remember the principle that the enemy must first be conquered then comes the prize. Many things cannot be had unless people go into battle.

Problems should to be looked at as doors of opportunity. They are opportunities for us to go in and gather up the spoils.

In 2 Chronicles chapter 20, verse 25, we read:

> *"And when Jehoshaphat and his people came to take away the spoil of them, they found among them in abundance both riches with the dead bodies, and precious jewels, which they stripped off for themselves, more than they could carry away: and they were three days in gathering of the spoil, it was so much."*

God will cause people to go into battle and strip their enemy of his goods. There are some enemies that God will tell us not to rebuke but to let into our lives. He may want to allow the stirring of some things so that we can get the spoils of victory. Every form of deliverance is not the same. At times, God wants us to permit the devil to come. We need to discern these kind of things by the Spirit of God.

STUDY QUESTIONS CHAPTER 10

1. _____ can also be used as spiritual songs.

2. Clever, skilled musicians were chosen or picked out by the _____ and instructed in the songs of the Lord.

3. As we bring forth our song, there will be a lifting of our _____ burden and a lifting up of _____ in our worship services.

4. _____ is the opposite of faith.

5. If we lack _____ of the contract [of our covenant with God], we will not know what we have a right to expect from God.

6. _____ was a sign of the covenant.

7. In a battle, it is essential that everyone know how to be a _____ that supplies.

8. When the priests went forward adorned in fine _____ and wearing precious _____ , they were making a statement to their enemies.

9. The Targums, an Aramaic translation of the Old Testament, indicates the belief that _____ angelic powers went into operation when they began to praise God.

10. After any spiritual battle we fight, we come out with _____ .

CHAPTER II

In the Old Testament, various expressions of praise are described. By studying the etymology of each related Hebrew word in the Strong's Exhaustive Concordance, we can identify the particular forms of praise.

TODAH PRAISE

The word "todah" or "todah praise" makes specific reference to a choir of worshippers. It means "to give thanks and praise for what God is going to do." Todah is a confession of faith. Once we understand God's purpose, we begin thanking Him for His plan. "Lord, I thank you that my mate is saved". "Father, I thank you that my children will be coming into the Kingdom and serving you."

Choirs, choreography, and processions are parts of "todah" praise. Often, people in a procession wave banners or flags. God wants to restore processions as a form of expression in worship.

In our country, we often have parades to celebrate special national holidays, such as Memorial Day and the Fourth of July. Often, the flag-bearers walk in front of the other marchers. Almost every nation on earth has some type of flag, and almost every flag has the color red on it somewhere. In the Bible, red is a color denoting blood and covenant. Our parades and flags are the world's versions of things God wants us to use in worshipping Him.

Todah is the "sacrifice of praise." When things look their worst and it looks as though all hell has broken out against us, that is the time to enter into a todah praise, lifting our hands to the Lord. Even when we do not feel like praising, God says to praise Him. In Psalm 50, verse 23, we read:

"Whoso offereth praise glorifieth me: and to him that ordereth his conversation aright will I show the salvation of God."

Note that the psalmist is referring to todah praise and that the word "conversation" does not mean speaking, but manner of life. Action must follow in accordance in praise. Having praised God for the salvation of a loved one, we must then affirm what we said by our actions towards that person.

I recall when I first obtained lucrative employment. I was getting married, so I decided to use "wisdom" in handling money. I stopped tithing and began putting away money for a rainy day, so that I could have something set aside when I started setting up a home. What happened? I suddenly lost my job. The point is that I had broken a covenant with God. My actions indicated that I expected to have a rainy day. I ceased to trust God for my daily needs. I thought I was to be wise and make sure that my future needs were going to be met.

In a related incident, I was talking with the pastor and an elder of a small church that had a congregation of about 300. In an area where there were churches attended by a thousand or more, their giving was at a high percentage. They not only met their own needs, but they gave much to outside ministries and missions. People were committed in that church. It grew and prospered because the principles of tithes and offerings were taught and followed.

I remember the pastor saying, "If someone went down and robbed a bank every week, would you allow him or her to be a member of your church?" I said, "No. Such an action would bring a reproach on the Kingdom of God." He then said, "Why do you allow them in the house of the Lord when they rob God week after week?"

Our priorities have been warped for a long time. In the Old Testament, the Israelites gave sacrificially to see that the temple, the House of the Lord, was built. Yet we, the Church of Jesus Christ, too often put giving last, and give from our left-overs. God is saying that if we would seek first the Kingdom of God and His righteousness, all these things would be added unto us (Matthew 6:33). We must keep our covenant with God and give of our time and money sacrificially.

Being about the Father's business involves making adjustments in our lives. Is the Kingdom of God truly first in our lives? Or is something else first? Are we on time for our jobs, yet late for worship service? Where are our priorities? Are we lacking things because God knows that we would waste and squander those things? God is going to put new and even greater demands on those who are moving with Him and truly seeking His Kingdom first.

BARAK PRAISE

Barak is a kind of praise meaning "to kneel and to bless as an act of adoration." In Judges 5:2, Deborah and Barak kneeled and blessed the Lord for avenging Israel in battle. This kind of praise speaks of reverence.

Reverence refers to a kind of fear, but not a fear that means that one is mortally terrified. God is re-establishing reverence both in His House and towards the things of God. In Scripture, we read of someone who was killed because he became too familiar with the Presence of God. This kind of familiarity can gradually happen to us. As we begin a new ministry, we might be up praying and praising in our homes asking God to bless what we are doing. Months later we might be so familiar with what we are doing that we become casual about it, or even irreverent. The value and worth can even be lost.

This can also happen with prophesying and moving in the Word of the Lord. We can become so familiar with the Presence of God and the glory of God that irreverence enters in. God is telling us to return to reverence in the Body of Christ.

Reverence for leadership is going to return in the church. When I was a child, we learned respect for those in authority. We would never have considered calling our pastor or an elderly person by his or her first name. Reverence and protocol are to be restored in God's house. (Refer to my book, Spiritual Protocol.)

Barak praise speaks of reverence and quietness before God, while expecting a response by faith. Of all the kinds of praise, this is the only one that includes silence. No statement about vocal expression is made. Barak praise is kneeling down in reverence before God. The outward bowing down shows the inward bowing of the heart. If the heart is not in submission and bowed down, it will be hard to bow down with submission in the external.

SHABAK PRAISE

Shabak praise means, "to address the Lord with a loud tune or a loud song." Psalm 117 says, "O praise the Lord, all ye nations: praise him, all ye people." The praise here is a shouting praise. God loves it when we shout praises. Quiet, shy people are not exempted from praising God in this way.

There are times when God wants all of us to shout His praises. There will be decency and order in this, for again, God is a God of order in all that He does. He sanctions the noise volume of this kind of praise, not because He is deaf or far removed from us, rather, His majesty and glory are worthy of the great and dramatic commendation of men and women.

Some trying situations that we might be in will not depart from us until we literally shout the praises of God. Often we are more comfortable with quietly praising the Lord. God sometimes wants us to get as excited about Him as we might get about a favorite sporting event or concert. When the half back rushes through the line and runs across the goal line in a championship football game, thousands rise to their feet shouting and rejoicing at victory for their team. How much more should we shout out the praises of our God, when He destroys the works of the enemy in our lives or there is some great spiritual victory in the Body of Christ.

In Luke chapter 19, verses 37-39, we read:
"And when he was come nigh, even now at the descent of the mount of Olives, the whole multitude of the disciples began to rejoice and praise God with a loud voice for all the mighty works that they had seen; Saying, Blessed be the King that cometh in the name of the Lord: peace in heaven, and glory in the highest. And some of the Pharisees from among the multitude said unto him, Master, rebuke thy disciples."

Those today who will not enter into Shabak praise have the same attitude as the Pharisees. They will become like the Sadducees (sad - you - sees!).

In Luke chapter 19, verse 40, Jesus answered the Pharisees:
"And he answered and said unto them, I tell you that, if these should hold their peace, the stones would immediately cry out."

Isn't it amazing that things in creation will do what they are supposed to do, while man might refuse!

Jesus clearly tells the Pharisees, "If the people around Me fail to praise Me, then the rocks will praise Me." As He continued He came upon Jerusalem. As he beheld the city with its destiny of destruction, His response was to weep. He then spoke over the city, telling of the coming judgment. The day would come when their enemies would come and surround them on every side.

In Luke chapter 19, verse 44, we read:

> *"And shall lay thee even with the ground, and thy children within thee; and they shall not leave in thee one stone upon another; because thou knewest not the time of thy visitation."*

If we do not know the time of God's visitation, destruction will come to our doors.

ZAMAR PRAISE

Zamar praise is "using musical instruments and song to worship God."

In Psalm 57, verse 7, we read:

> *"My heart is fixed, O God, my heart is fixed: I will sing and give praise."*

Zamar praise is often done using string instruments. As the musicians pull upon the strings of their instruments, they begin to pull upon the heart strings of the people. When David pulled down the strings of his harp, he pulled upon the heart of Saul and Saul was turned into another man. (I Samuel 18:10.)

There is clearly more than one way to cast out a devil and bring about deliverance. Some fairly recent movies have depicted lengthy and quite violent deliverance, in which people became sick and expectorate green vomit.

Yet, I have observed two other kinds of deliverance. The first is by correction. If a child needs deliverance, there is the rod of correction. Scripture tells us that the rod of correction will drive out the foolishness which is bound in the heart of a child. (Proverbs 22:15)

Another way of deliverance is through music. That's why we must be selective about the music we listen to. Scientists have placed plants in a room where loud, hard, rock music was played constantly. The plants died.

Many of us are deceived into thinking that it is not the music that is wrong, just the words in the songs. Actually, the music itself has an effect. Can plants understand the words of a song? The sound of the music is what killed them. God doesn't want us to get the music of the world and put His Words to it. The world should be copying us, not us copying the world. We should set the pace.

HALEL PRAISE

"Halel" means " to get foolish for God." Halel praise refers to "praise which shines forth fearlessly with foolish exuberance." This is the most common word for praise in the Scripture. From it comes the imperative word "Hallelujah", which means "Praise the Lord." It is praise by boosting , by celebrating, or by raving about Him until it seems foolish. That's just the way God wants us to praise Him.

In 1 Chronicles chapter 16, verse 4, we read:

"And be appointed certain of the Levites to minister before the ark of the LORD, and to record, and to thank and praise the LORD God of Israel"

Some were appointed to act foolish before the God of Israel. There were appointed people who would move about in unashamed praise, without care of what others might think of them.

It is wonderful to be excited about Jesus and the Word of God. We need to worship Him without shame and with exuberance. God is bringing forth people who will make a joyful sound unto the Lord and get clamorously foolish before God.

A PROPHETIC WORD: GIVEN IN 1986

"A generation of men and women is going to come forth...."

The Word of the Lord came to me saying: "For behold there is a generation of men and women that is going to come forth in an hour, that you know not of . For yea, they are going to begin to move in great boldness and in great strength, such as you've never seen or witnessed before. It shall be a generation which is going to hit the streets, and they are going to understand the purposes of the Kingdom. They are going to say that the Kingdom of God suffereth violence, and the violent begin to take it by force.

I am going to bring forth a group of young men and women in this day who are going to move in unashamed praise," saith the Lord. "They will begin to hit the streets, and they will drag the fish in, even if they do not want to jump into the net. For you see, I am going to bring forth a harvest in this day such as you've never seen and as you've never witnessed."

"They will compel them to come. For in days gone by men would beseech them, and cry, "Would you like to receive Jesus?" But you are going to find that this is the day when they

will not have a choice, but they will be compelled to come into my Kingdom.

This will be a time when the Gospel shall be known as the power of God unto salvation. For you have not foreseen the degree of power that I want to bring forth, and that is because you have not truly believed the reality of My Gospel. Yet My Gospel of the Kingdom is going to literally cause nations to fall on their faces," saith God.

Watch Me begin to move in this day and in this hour. I'm going to move in your political arena. I'm moving in the White House, and I'm walking down the corridors. for did I not tell thee that this would be a year of shame for this nation, saith God? Did I not tell thee that this would be a year of the changing of the guard, saith God? But yea, you have not seen anything yet compared to that which I'm going to bring forth.

But yea, you shall see the Church come into a period of many scandals. Many hidden events will begin to surface, saith the Lord, and I'm going to begin to move upon the oriental nations. You are going to begin to find them rising up power in degrees that thou hast never seen or ever known. For I am going to cause great changes to take place nationwide.

This will be the time of mocking, whereby there shall be great pressure as has never been seen before. For yea, I am going to allow a great intensity to begin to take place in this nation concerning racism, and you haven't seen anything yet, for you thought the sixties were something. You will not have seen anything until you have seen the nineties.

There will be a great rising up, and there shall be much blood that shall be shed, in the streets. I am going to cause these things to come to pass. This will begin to take place nationally, I'm going to move among the South Africans in a way and in a degree such as you have never seen.

'I'm going to raise up a leader, even in this nation who is going to begin to have a voice, and you are going to find that the prophets of God are going to hit your senators and congressmen with he Word of the Lord. I'm going to cause those who will not hear My Word to be yanked and moved out of offices immediately.

This will be the time, that I am going to set the stage. I'm moving into the school system, and the educational department. I'm going to cause a change even in thy mayor, there is going to be a great stir as has never been before.

This will be the time, that as you will begin to see the cycle roll, you're going to begin to see great turns, and even the financial situation shall begin to feel the pressure by the end of 1999. You're going to begin to see the mask of uncertainty covering the faces of financial leaders.

This will be the time, that it will be My people who will hold the key. It will be My people who will understand the timetable. It will be My people who will receive of the spirit of Issachar. And yea, they shall know what to do as the time begins to arise. For I am going to begin to move and this will be the time of the mocking of My Spirit.

For great will be the revival that shall take place in Catholicism, I am going to begin to cause that branch to rise up. It will seem as though she will become a voice even unto this nation, I'll allow it because My people would not move into that place and into that function.

But, it shall begin to provoke many to jealousy: they are going to begin to have a voice in their cities and in their communities, for this will be the time of the changes that are going to begin to take place. This will the time of the setting of the stage of new individuals who are going to begin to rise up.

You're going to begin to find that even concerning the religious scandals that have been taking place, there are a host of ministries which you have not heard of that are even a part of that. But yea, will I not cause the covers to begin to be pulled back?

Even as the Church shall walk in much shame, saith God, yea, watch Me begin to take her from the shame and raise her up to a place of honor. For yea, will I not bring My people back down to their knees, saith God?

Will I not begin to cause the radio and the television media to be closed unto them? But only to reopen it so that my people can begin to return back unto the local Church. For

I'm going to do a quick work. The day of substitution is over. The Church is coming into an hour of representing My Authority, saith the Lord.

TEHILLAH PRAISE

Tehilla praise is "a laudation, or a hymn." It differs from the other forms of praise in that while the other realms of praise involve faith, this word implies that God has responded to that faith. It means "He literally inhabits the praise and is enthroned in the midst of the Tehillah." God is enthroned upon the Tehilla praises of Israel. There is an actual manifestation of that which you have praised God for in faith. God comes down and manifests Himself in the praise.

We must learn how to wait in praise. As we praise God and make our confessions, we need to wait and allow God to come down and manifest Himself. Too often we've been in praise services where we keep going and going, never waiting for the manifestation of God.

Church services, even non-denominational churches, are often too formulated. The scripture does not order the church services to begin with praise and worship followed by the sermon. Yet, many churches keep this pattern. For instance, praise and worship can easily be extended into the time of the offering, which is the giving back to God of what he has given us strength to accumulate from week to week.

HYMNS

Hymns denote "songs of praise addressed to God."

In Ephesians chapter 5, verses 19-22, we read:
> *"Speaking to yourselves in psalms and hymns and spiritual songs, singing and making melody in your heart to the Lord; Giving thanks always for all things unto God and the Father in the name of our Lord Jesus Christ; Submitting yourselves one to another in the fear of God. Wives, submit yourselves unto your own husbands, as unto the Lord."*

Notice that Paul goes from talking about the praise of God to talking about the relationship of husbands and wives.

In Colossians chapter 3, verses 16-18, we read:
> *"Let the word of Christ dwell in you richly in all wisdom; teaching and admonishing one another in psalms and hymns and spiritual songs, singing with grace in your hearts to the Lord. And whatsoever ye do in word or deed, do all in the name of the Lord Jesus,*

giving thanks to God and the Father by him. Wives, submit yourselves unto your own husbands, as it is fit in the Lord."

There is soon to be a time when it will be the norm for musicians in the church to come forth and sing special songs to members of the congregation. The world has taken over what God had intended for His people.

Notice that the call to praise God is followed by instructions to husbands and wives. A relationship must be vertical before it can be horizontal. If a man cannot relate and be open to God, he will not be able to relate and be open to his mate.

In many instances, the emotions of men have been frozen. As children, they were taught to be unemotional, to never show their emotions by crying or any other outward display. They've been taught to conceal and deny any emotional response. That's why many men fail to enter into the full expression of worship. Their attitude is, "Let the women pray to the Lord and give thanks to God. I'm standing over here. Praise God."

In Israel, the men led the worship. They led the dance. Certain dancers, such as the war dances, were reserved exclusively for the men. If we pulled men forward to dance in church today, many would strongly resist. God is telling us that if our relationship is not right vertically [with Him], we are never going to be able to relate correctly [horizontally] with our mate.

We must learn how to enter into a proper vertical relationship with the Lord. We will be able to learn how to relate to each other in a proper way. Many Christians are not properly relating to one another. Some people have been so hurt in relationships with others that they will attend a church, and give their offering, but they will now allow themselves to become a part of the Body. "I've been hurt by churches too much," they say. "I won't get involved like that again!"

The Bible talks about the assembling together of believers (Hebrews 10:25). This is akin to having pieces of a piano lying about a room scattered, but not assembled. For that piano to be assembled, hands have to be laid on it. This is true about assembling anything. In too many of our churches, we have a gathering together of people, but no assembly. Just like a piano, sometimes when we want to move from gathering together to assembling, it takes a little hammering and banging them into place.

Perhaps it is time to exert some force to truly begin assembling together as the Lord would have us to. Otherwise, our churches would be just like that unassembled piano; something with the potential to produce beautiful and pleasing melodies, yet essentially totally useless in its present state.

It is highly significant that in Ephesians chapter 5, Paul connects the singing of hymns with the action of submitting to one another. Praise involves more than just making a melody in our hearts. It involves an action of our being. It involves surrendering ourselves collectively to the purpose and the plan of the One to whom we are singing and making melody. Praise involves giving of ourselves, willingly even one to another, as He gave Himself willingly for each of us!

STUDY QUESTIONS CHAPTER II

1. Todah praise means "to give thanks and praise for what God is _____ to do.

2. We, the Church of Jesus Christ too often put giving last and give from our _____.

3. Barak praise speaks of _____.

4. Shabbak praise is a _____.

5. Zamar praise is often done using _____.

6. _____ praise refers to praise which shines forth fearlessly and with foolish exuberance.

7. Tehillah praise differs from the other forms of praise in that while the other forms of praise involve _____, this word implies that God has _____ to that faith.

8. _____ denotes "songs of praise addressed to God."

9. A _____ must be vertical, before it can be horizontal.

10. In too many of our churches, we have a gathering together of people, but no ____.

CHAPTER 12

Psalms 8 has some important and significant things to say about praise and worship:

"O LORD our Lord, how excellent is thy name in all the earth! who hast set thy glory above the heavens. Out of the mouth of babes and sucklings hast thou ordained strength because of thine enemies, that thou mightest still the enemy and the avenger.
When I consider thy heavens, the work of thy fingers, the moon and the stars, which thou hast ordained; What is man, that thou art mindful of him? and the son of man, that thou visitest him? For thou hast made him a little lower than the angels, and hast crowned him with glory and honor. Thou madest him to have dominion over works of thy hands: thou hast put all things under his feet: All sheep and oxen, yea, and the beasts of the field; The fowl of the air, and the fish of the sea, and whatsoever passeth through the paths of the seas. O LORD our Lord, how excellent is thy name in all the earth!"

In praise, we can express ourselves unto God. As we learned in the previous lesson, there are many ways to praise God including: shouting, kneeling, singing, dancing, and being clamorously foolish. Praise stills the hand of the enemy. When we learn how to praise, we will come under the order of God.

Yawdah praise refers to "praise in the stretching forth of our hands." The Lord will teach our hands how to war and our fingers to fight. (Psalms 144, verse 1.) Banners will return to the House of the Lord. They will be artistically designed testimonies of what God is doing. They will denote His Nature. There will be processions in the House of the Lord, with people carrying banners.

Notice Psalms 8 opens with "O Lord our Lord." In the Hebrew, this is Jehovah Adoneynu, which means "Lord or Master." This is Jehovah, who is our sovereign Lord and Master. The Psalmist David opens with this powerful word of reference. We who have learned to call God "Abba, Father," are not being called to reverence God as our Lord and Master. We must enter into His Presence with reverence.

David is writing a song to God. He is the shepherd boy. He has an observant eye of the works of God in the heavens above and on the earth below. He notices the works of God's Hands. God sometimes wants us to take notice of what He is saying and doing. We may need to look up into the heavens and say, "Lord, I thank You for the sun. I thank You for the moon that gives us light by night." Sometimes we take the air for granted. "Lord, I thank You for the oxygen and the nitrogen in the air."

When we think we don't have much to praise God for, we can say, "Lord, I thank You for the life which You have given me. Lord, I thank You for what You have done in my life."

We need to get caught up in what God is doing for us. We need to think of the goodness of Jesus and to take a moment out of the day to say, "Lord, I thank You." Thank God for whatever you have. Thank Him for your ability of speech.

Many Christians speak of going before God and more or less telling Him what needs to be accomplished. Sometimes, they even tell God that they need things done in a certain number of days. God wants to bring us back out of the relationship of calling Him "Daddy," to an understanding that He is still Father. Any extreme is bad. We need to come into the fullness of truth of what God is saying.

When I come into the Presence of god, I come in reverence to Him. I say, "Lord, I have no rights. I am Your servant. I am only here to hear what You want me to represent and to perform Your will on earth." We should remember the prayer of Jesus which said, "Thy kingdom come, Thy will be done on earth as it is in heaven."

Is the will of God in heaven sickness? No Then the will of God on earth is not sickness, but health. Is the will of God in heaven poverty? No! Then the will of God on earth is not poverty, but prosperity.

Sometimes we hear people say that those in ministry are making "too much money." How can we make too much money? Money comes from God. How can we have too much of what belongs to God? The world has taught us that preachers of the gospel should remain poor, so that they might remain humble. The same world teaches and accepts that an actor or an actress, a sports figure or a corporate executive, can and should make millions of dollars. How much more should men and women who are doing God's work on earth be compensated by their Heavenly Employer?

When I was growing up, if the pastor got a new car, some people in the congregation got nervous. Pastors and their families were routinely given hand-me-down clothing. They weren't expected to be able to buy new things. An austere, near poverty lifestyle was more or less expected of them. This was the mentality of the church.

God is saying that day is over. He is saying that the day is coming when His people will look the best and dress the best. The world will not be the pacesetter. The Church will be the pacesetter and the standard which God will use to declare His glory. David looked at the heavens and the earth and cried out to God saying, "How excellent [how glorious] is thy name." We need to learn how to worship and praise the Name of Jesus. We read in Acts 2:21: "... whosoever shall call on the name of the Lord shall be saved." Calling upon the Name of Jesus brings deliverance. If we have poverty, sickness or any infirmity, we need to call upon the Name of Jesus.

Note that it is one thing to say the Name, and another thing to call the Name. When we call the Name of Jesus, He comes upon the scene. We are welcome in His Kingdom. When we do not speak and declare the Name of Jesus in our lives, we fail to worship that Name.

STILLING THE HAND OF THE ENEMY

In Psalms 8, verse 2, David talks about strength coming even from babes and sucklings to still the enemy. We know that praise will still the hand of the enemy, and lack of praise will still the Hand of God. As long as I praise God, my enemy is paralyzed. When I stop praising Him, I give God no room to move. Since God inhabits the praises of His people, it is essential that we create an atmosphere of praise in which He can dwell. That's why the enemy likes to keep us depressed and oppressed.

David says in Psalms 8, that even as children praise and dance before the Lord, the hand of the enemy is stilled. Children praise God with pure motives. The praise of children declares the power that is ascribed to God. God uses the mouth of children against those who oppose the revelation of God.

Often, adults praise God "because ..." Our motives are impure; we want something from God. Sometimes we even go on a fast of our own choosing. We may think we are honoring God by this. In reality, our motive is to twist the arm of God, get His immediate attention, and persuade Him to say "yes" to our request. A person should fast when God ordains and moves upon him or her to do so.

Often, fasting will shut down the flesh so that the spirit can ascend. Even in the natural, if a person goes on a very restricted diet and eats only vegetables and fruits or drinks only juices, that person will naturally become more alert. They're not as sluggish and will respond quicker. Fasting should come from obedience and a desire to represent the Kingdom of God. God will move heaven and earth because we have made this our choice.

God uses the weak things to confound the wise.
In 1 Corinthians chapter 1, verses 22-27, we read:

"For the Jews require a sign, and the Greeks seek after wisdom: But we preach Christ crucified, unto the Jews a stumblingblock, and unto the Greeks foolishness; But unto them which are called, both Jews and Greeks, Christ the power of God, and the wisdom of God. Because the foolishness of God is wiser than men; and the weakness of God is stronger than men. For ye see your calling, brethren, how that not many wise men after the flesh, not many mighty, not many noble, are called: But God hath chosen the foolish things of the world to confound the wise; and God hath chosen the weak things of the world to confound the things which are mighty;"

I can't explain how a flower has the strength to break through the ground. It is so tender and weak, yet it comes up. God will take the weak things to confound what is mighty. I can't explain that. God will often take people who are uneducated and send them to those who are educated. He'll take the foolish and weak things to confound those who are mighty.

GOD AND MAN

In Psalms 8, verses 4 and 5, we read:

"What is man, that thou art mindful of him? and the son of man, that thou visitest him? For thou hast made him a little lower than the angels, and hast crowned him with glory and honor."

The word "angels" is the Hebrew word; "ELOHIM," which means "God." Perhaps when the translators worked with the original text, they could not deal with the idea that God would make man a little lower than God. They may have then put in the word, "angels" instead.

The psalmist may very well have been looking back at creation.
In Genesis chapter 1, verses 26-28, we read:

"And God said, Let us make man in our image, after our likeness: and let them have dominion over the fish of the sea, and over the fowl of the air, and over the cattle, and over all the earth, and over every creeping thing that creepeth upon the earth. So God created man in his own image, in the image of God created he him; male and female created he them. And God blessed them, and God said unto them, Be fruitful, and multiply, and replenish the earth, and subdue it: and have dominion over the fish of the sea, and over the fowl of the air, and over every living thing that moveth upon the earth."

God wanted man to be in such a place that when He looked at man He would see Himself. The job of the church is to restore the Godly image of man. God wants a Church which will represent His Kingdom. The power of God will be so restored within the Church because of authority and submission. When an individual begins to step out of line or overreach their boundaries, we will see the chastisement of God manifested amongst us. People's hearts will begin to prick them. The church will cease from becoming a circus, in which anything that goes on is all right.

There will no longer be anarchy. The depth of our relationship with God will be the degree that God will deal with us. The deeper we get into the things of God, great will be the demands placed upon us. We will find God demanding more of our time. We will learn how to take Jesus shopping with us. We will hear Him tell us what to buy and what not to buy. Have you ever bought something after hearing the Holy Spirit tell you not to? Perhaps you then saw the same item somewhere else at a cheaper price. Maybe you went home and realized that it wasn't something you truly needed or even wanted.

Any time you feel pressured to do something, you shouldn't do anything. Decisions made under pressure will always be wrong decisions. The psalmist also says that man was "crowned with glory and honor." In this Scripture, man begins to transcend even the angels, for man is the only creature upon which God has placed a crown. Man is to be the ruler here on earth, under God.

THE LAW OF DOMINION

The law of Dominion states: Whatsoever I do not have dominion over, it has dominion over me. For instance, if a person does not have dominion over cigarettes, then cigarettes will have dominion over him. Similarly, a person can be enslaved by alcohol or by an ungodly relationship. People sometimes become involved in relationships with those who are unsaved. They try to convince themselves that it is all right.

"After we are married, I know he (she) will love me enough that he will want to be saved." It simply doesn't work that way! Ask any believer you know who is married to an unsaved person, and they will tell you what it is like.

Even if someone comes to the church and gets saved, there needs to be some caution and wisdom. A year should pass before there is courtship and marriage. Time is needed to see if the person's salvation is tangible. We need to see if there is godly fruit being manifested in that person's life. Evidence of the fruits of the Spirit of God in a person's life indicates a true and abiding walk with the Lord.

The place of man's dominion is on earth. We do not have dominion in heaven. The extent of a man's dominion is only on the earth. Even there, it is limited only to the different classes of creatures in the regions of the land, air and sea.

In verses 6 and 7 of Psalms 8, the psalmist places domesticated animals first, as being most completely under man's dominion. The list then moves to animals in the wilderness. When a person begins to appreciate the authority he has, he will first experience it within his home environment. Thus, we might feel quite comfortable that our pet dog and/or cat is well trained and obedient. It is another thing for us to go out into the jungle and think that lions, tigers or bears will be obedient to us.

Man is not only to have dominion; in Genesis, he is commanded to subdue the earth. The commission thus received was for man to utilize, for his necessities, the vast resources of the earth. We are to move in the fields of agriculture, oceanography, geology, and science. People of God will be given wisdom in these fields.

There are cures for cancer and for AIDS in the earth. We need to be in a place where the world will look to us for solutions to problems and crises. They need to see that the church has the answer and the key. Years ago, those making decisions in government would first go and seek the counsel of religious leaders. They wanted to know whether those decisions were godly or ungodly. Today, they don't even hear the church, much less consult with it.

Judgment begins first at the House of God. That means that the church is going to begin making statements. When they do this, the world is going to have to come into alignment with those statements.

Psalms 8, verse 9, reads:
"O LORD our Lord, how excellent is thy name in all the earth!"

A PRAYER OF PRAISE AND THANKSGIVING

We need to thank God for all the things in Psalms 8. We need to thank God for being God.

Magnify the Lord, Magnify the Lord!
We love You Lord.
We thank You Lord for the food on the table.
We thank You Lord for the clothes on our backs.
We thank You Lord for the sunshine and the rain.
We thank You Lord for being God, all by Yourself.
For being God, all by Yourself.
We thank You Lord. We thank you Lord. We thank You Lord.
O Praise the Lord. O thank the Lord, for being God.
We thank You Lord.

STUDY QUESTIONS CHAPTER 12

1. In praise, we can _____ ourselves to God.
2. _____ praise refers to praise in the stretching forth of our hands.
3. The will of God on earth is not sickness, but _____; not _____ , but prosperity.
4. A person should _____ when God ordains and moves upon him or her to do so.
5. God will take the _____ and_____ things to confound those who are mighty.
6. God wanted man to be in such a place that when He looked at man He would see _____ .
7. The degree of depth in our _____ with God will be the _____ degree with which God deals with us.
8. Any time you're _____ to make a decision, you will always make the wrong decision.
9. The _____ states: Whatsoever I do not have dominion over, has dominion over me.
10. The commission thus receiving Genesis was for man to utilize, for his necessities, the _____ of the earth.

CHAPTER 13

Psalms 1 begins:

> *"BLESSED is the man that walketh not in the counsel of the ungodly, nor standeth in the way of sinners, nor sitteth in the seat of the scornful."*

When Jesus had to deal with complex or confrontational situations, He answered a question with a question. Thus, He left people with something to think about. God will give us wisdom concerning how to answer certain statements. A righteous man, one who will be blessed, will not find his place in the company of scorners. When such a person is in the presence of a righteous man, they will cease from their scorning. Often, they will simply back away when they see a godly person coming.

Psalms 1 continues:

> *"But his delight is in the law of the LORD; and in his law doth he meditate day and night."*

Delight means "great joy or extreme pleasure." Man's delight is in the law, meaning not just the law of Moses, but all the ways of God. Our delight should be in the scriptures. We should have a love for the Word of God such that we look forward to seeing what the Word has to say regarding our lives. We need to be excited about understanding the ways of God.

We don't want to be people who just know God's acts. The Bible tells us that the children of Israel knew God's acts, but Moses knew His ways. God wants to take us from a place of testimony, hearing of the mighty acts of God, to one of learning and understanding the ways of the Lord.

LORD, HELP ME TO LEARN AND UNDERSTAND THY WAYS

When we understand the ways of God, we'll know the things we can and cannot do. There are certain things parents do not have to say to their children. The children quickly learn and discern that certain things simply won't be liked or tolerated. "I've never heard mom say that we can't do that ... but I've been around her long enough to know that she won't like it!"

We learn a person's ways by being around them. Moses spent time with God. If we spend time in the Father's Presence, we will learn some of Father's ways, then when we are in situations where people are asking us to go out with them or do certain things, we'll hear the Holy Spirit telling us, "No, no." You'll be able to say, "I've been around Father long enough to know that isn't the right thing to do."

We'll see an outfit in the store and really want to buy it. When we try on the outfit, finding it to be a little tight and revealing in some spots, the Holy Spirit will quicken unto us that this is not the outfit to buy. We may argue, "Yes, I know it's a little tight, but maybe God won't be displeased with it too much." After awhile, we will simply know what God will like and what He won't.

I've been in churches where the preacher spent a whole hour talking against lipstick, makeup and certain kinds of clothing. Meanwhile, people were there with cancers, terrible problems, and serious questions about the gospel. They were not getting fed. One denomination told women that they could not wear pants or shave their legs. This was due to a Scripture stating it was a sin and abomination for a woman to cut her hair and wear men's apparel.

When I started in ministry, one of the many things the Holy Spirit told me: "Let me do my job, and you do your job. Let me do the convicting. I'll teach the people how to dress. You win the soul and let me deal with the clothes." If you introduce people to Jesus properly, you'll get them into a working relationship with the Lord. When they go to the store, God will go with them and the Holy Spirit will teach them how to dress.

PERSECUTION AND AFFLICTION

One thing I've noticed, when you begin to teach on a particular area, it is almost certain there's going to be a testing in that area. Jesus taught His disciples valuable lessons on faith. Afterward, everyone boarded a boat and set sail. As the storm began to arise with the threat of death and destruction, they cried out in complete terror. All the powerful teachings on faith were forgotten! When we have our greatest victories in the Spirit, we need to get ready for our greatest tests. Pastors are not immune to these trials and testings. Oftentimes, the members of the congregation will call the pastor on the phone for counsel when they are under trials and testings. Meanwhile, the pastor also may be under testing and wonder whom he or she might call!

PERSECUTION AND AFFLICTION ARRIVE FOR THE WORD'S SAKE

When we are in a church where the Word of God is coming forth, we are also going to have heavy trials. When we learn something in school, we have a test to see whether we have mastered it. After Jesus taught the disciples, they went through a time of testing. Jesus fell asleep in the boat and the storm started brewing. Water was coming into their boat.

I recall visiting an island where all of us were out on the water in a glass-bottomed boat. The sea became a bit rough, and I wasn't too happy about what was going on! Water was coming into the boat! I got a glimpse of what it must have been like for the disciples. Then, it was much worse. It was nighttime and dark. Water was pouring into their boat. A storm was raging with tides up to fifty feet.

During the testing, no one thought of the teachings in the gospels: "All you need is faith the size of a grain of mustard seed." They shouted out, "Master, don't you care that we perish?" They were fearful. They were so afraid, they shook Jesus to awaken Him. He simply said, "Peace be still." It doesn't matter how high our waves are, the Master is still on board. He has given us the authority to say, "Peace be still."

Recently, I was going through some trials and came upon an interesting book. They defined "determination" as: "understanding that our present struggles are preparing us for our future achievements." As I thought about that, I recalled the butterfly and the moth; a story about how a little boy tried to help a butterfly free itself from its cocoon. He broke open the cocoon to make it easier for the butterfly to emerge. Then he stood by and watched, expecting that the butterfly would start to fly. Of course, it never did. It died.

The butterfly had not passed through the cocoon stage. It hadn't experienced its present struggle. Because it hadn't broken through the cocoon on its own strength, its wings were not strong enough to take flight. The struggle to get through the cocoon strengthens the butterfly's wings for the achievement of flight.

The struggles we are in prepares us for our future achievements and goals, being specifically designed. It's the same thing for a chick inside an egg. If we were to break open the egg for it instead of letting it peck its way out, the chick would not survive. It could not live in the atmosphere outside the egg. It is the struggle to peck its way out of the egg that gives the chick the ability to survive outside.

Some people may have thought that when they came to Jesus, they would have no more struggles or problems. If someone told you that, the statement is wrong! When we come to the Lord, that is when the struggle begins. He wants to strengthen our wings so that we will fly one day. He wants to teach us to come out of our own circumstances by His ability so we can move on to new stages and levels.

Most of us want our miracle. We want Jesus to send an angel to break open the cocoon or the eggshell and set us free from whatever is trying us. Yet, God leaves us in some circumstances, deliberately letting us stay there and cook for awhile. We need to rejoice, even under pressure and say, "Lord, I thank you, for you are preparing me for my future achievements."

I know from experience that when we get too comfortable and secure in a place, God will often begin to remove us from that place. He will push us towards where He wants us to be. Sometimes He will even "kick" us a little bit to get us moving. It was that way when I moved out to pastor a church. This was not my choice, but God's.

It is easy to praise God when we are in our comfort zone. We may even begin to judge those who are not able to praise so easily. When we dislocate from our comfortable spot, when things are not going our way or direct attacks come against us, it takes faith to lift up our hands and say, "Thank you Jesus."

MEDITATION

According to Strong's Exhaustive Concordance "meditation" means "to mutter to oneself." This is a quick course on meditation. How many of us know how to worry? Meditation is simply "worrying" God's promises.

A person deposits a check in their checking account, then they get on a commuter train or bus to go to work. They sit there not knowing or caring who is sitting around them. It could be the President of the United States, the Governor or even someone's pet dog. This person doesn't know or care. Their mind is on their checkbook. "Which bill can I send out? I wonder what will happen if I don't send this check right now?" Their mind clicks away like a calculator.

Many of us have been in a situation like that. That is meditation. The person is meditating on numbers and figures, rolling them round and round in their mind, hoping that they will obtain the solution to their dilemma.

The person in our story arrives at work, perhaps doing their job, but not really concentrating on the business at hand. They continue to meditate on their problem. Their mind will recall another bill which they'd forgotten about that morning. "How can I make things balance?" They may even say a prayer, "Lord Jesus, you've got to help me!" As they continue to think about the bills, the stack seems to grow higher and higher.

Worrying is a negative form of meditation. We need to get to where we meditate God's way. Instead of focusing on our problems, we should think about the promises of God. We will then start to feel lighter and more joyful. Our delight will then be in the law of the Lord, and we will find ourselves meditating upon His Word day and night. When we think about things, such as money problems, we take them to sleep with us. We may have dreams that cause frustration. Suppose we dream that we have an abundance of money, only to wake up to our empty bank account? Does this cause your day to begin with frustration and disappointment? Of course! How much better to take thoughts of Jesus with us into our sleep. We will then awake refreshed. Meditation on Him will cause us to have dreams in which we prophesy, cast out devils or speak in tongues. We will be literally meditating upon the Lord, even in our sleep.

We shall become like the person in Psalms 1 verse 3, when meditating day and night.
> *"And he shall be like a tree planted by the rivers of water, that bringeth forth his fruit in*
> *his season; his leaf also shall not wither; and whatsoever he doeth shall prosper."*

PLANTED BY THE LORD

Notice the word planted. We need to remember that the Lord plants us, and we are not cast down. A tree doesn't plant itself, someone else plants it. In our case, the Lord plants us. He directs us to places and plants us there to take root.

If I move a plant, it has to go with me. The plant really can't say that it doesn't want to go. It is in the mover's hands. We really need to be like it. When God says "Move," we need to move!

At times we say things like, "Lord, you can't mean I should go to that church. It's 20 miles away. There are at least 10 churches closer to me than that one;" to which the Lord might well reply, "I know that."

We don't always understand the ways of God. If Abraham had gone to the wrong mountain to sacrifice his son, there could not have been a ram waiting in the bush for him. Sometimes our prayers are not answered because we are in the wrong place. God told Elijah to go to the brook Cherith. (1 Kings 17.) Elijah could have made excuses for himself. He could have justified his disobedience and gone somewhere else, missing the raven that God sent to him to provide his food.

Sometimes we stand in the way of good things coming to us. We need to be where God told us to be so that we might receive His provision.

Notice, the psalmist says that the fruit will come up "in due season." We might sow and not see any fruit for a long time. Fruit doesn't grow immediately. It takes time. When I was a child, I used to plant seeds on my grandmother's farm. I'd then go out every other day or so and check to see if anything was growing yet. Some of us are like that. "Lord, I have given and given, yet I see no fruit from my giving."

We may even be tempted to dig up the seeds that we have planted. Digging up seeds, of course, kills the plant. We need simply to give and forget it. We need to let our seeds die. As real seeds die (or break open), the plants begin to grow. That is the way it is with spiritual seeds also.

Some types of vegetation, like potatoes, stay buried in the earth. In like manner, some of our treasures stay buried inside of us. God will teach us wisdom, showing us how to draw out these treasures. We are assured that we will bear fruit in our proper season. Therefore, we are to be patient and continue to sow. Eventually, our fruit will come forth. Of course, if we haven't sown, then nothing will come forth.

Man will tell us that it is crazy to give so much into the church and into missions and ministries. God will tell us that it is wise to follow His precepts and His example. In doing so, He will prosper and bless us, but only when we do things according to His pattern. He will teach us to be givers in His Kingdom.

In Psalms 1, the planted tree by the river can draw life and freshness from an unfailing source. The Scripture also tells us "our leaf shall not wither." Wither means "to shrivel or shrink." A plant exposed to too much heat or cold, will shrivel or dry up. If we walk in God's principles, we will be as an evergreen tree. God will cause the foliage to always be there, in order for us to stand in the Father's Presence; where He has planted us.

In Psalms 1, verses 4-6, we read:

"The ungodly are not so: but are like the chaff which the wind driveth away." Therefore the ungodly shall not stand in the judgment, nor sinners in the congregation of the righteous. For the LORD knoweth the way of the righteous: but the way of the ungodly shall perish."

Chaff is something that is weak or worthless. In ancient times, it was of no value. When they winnowed the corn, they would throw it into the air and the wind would blow the chaff away. The Bible says that the wicked are like the chaff. When God comes, the Holy Spirit blows. The chaff are blown away while only the righteous remain. Scripture tells us that the righteous shall never be moved. We are not going to "get out of here." There is an old familiar song: "I shall not be moved. Like a tree planted by the water, I shall not be moved."

Some people are always moving. They go from church to church. A tree does not move easily. God will cause us to be like trees, planted with roots that will grow deeper. We will learn how to weather the storms. When problems come, we won't just pack up and move away. We will recall that the Scripture says, "For My yoke is easy, and My burden is light" (Matthew 11:30). God wants us to know that we have His ability and power to weather the storms of life.

The wicked shall not stand. The ungodly shall perish. We need to understand planting and stability. I learned early that I didn't have my own ministry. My ministry was to the House of the Lord. It was for blessing the Body of Christ. I was to move according to God's timing and God's purpose. If we do that, God will not cause us to be ashamed. If we move on our own will, we will become unstable.

Sometimes a person will come to a church with "their" ministry. They won't have the vision of the House. The vision of the House can be explained like this: suppose an architect-designer was hired to design a new kitchen. Then, someone else comes to that home where he has started building. They have good ideas, lots of zeal and enthusiasm, and truly want to help. Yet, they don't have any idea or sense of what the architect has designed or planned. With that thought, they begin installing a fancy bathroom right in the center of the kitchen. The result: utter confusion! There is a stench in the kitchen! Things become built according to two different visions. Something is clearly out of order.

How often has the local church experienced this phenomena? Many wounds suffered by the Body of Christ are unnecessary if people understood the principle of having the vision of the house. Good ideas don't qualify ministry. We must allow God to cause our gift to make room for us and bring us before great men. God plants the seed of a dream in you for an aspect of ministry. Your duty is to allow your ambition to die and allow God to open the door in His time. When attempting to build our own vision, without understanding the vision of the House, we're doing the same thing as the over-zealous young architect. We end up building toilets in the kitchen.

A PRAYER OF THANKSGIVING AND PETITION

Father, I want to be the planting of the Lord:

Lord, I want to withstand trials, struggles, and persecution. I want to have the ability to weather the storm, Lord. Only You can help me. Lord, I give myself unto You, in spite of what it may cost. I know everything comes with a price. I know wisdom comes with a price. Experience is costly. Father, I'm learning to thank You for every trying moment! Lord I know that the trying of my faith will work out Your patience and purpose in me. Patience, Lord I want patience to have her perfect work in my life. Lord, I want to be properly joined, properly related, growing in Your strength and growing in Your grace. Lord, help me today to stand and when I've done all to stand; I know that Your Word tells me just to stand. Lord, give me the endurance today.

A MESSAGE FROM THE LORD

"Father, I don't understand why my household this day is so chaotic. It seems like there are reports from others about how God is saving in their homes, but my household still seems filled with confusion. Lord, I just want to walk away. Let me just get a small apartment."

The Lord says to you, this day, when you've done all, to stand. STAND!! "Lord, I'm tired of my job. They don't recognize me there. In fact, they didn't give me my last raise. They don't appreciate me there. I want to leave."

Yet, God hasn't told you to go. When you've done all, to stand; God says, STAND! For His grace is sufficient for thee, and His strength is made perfect in times of need. For the Lord says He will help you, and He will see you through. You just yield to the planting of the Lord." To another, He is saying: "It is time for you to move on." Yet, He wants you to wait for His timetable, for He'll show you how He is to plant you. For there are many who move in haste, not understanding the timetable of the Lord. In their haste to move, they make unwise decisions and the purposes of God do not get fulfilled in their lives. Yet, the Lord says when you've done all to stand today, you are to stand. STAND!!

A PRAYER OF PRAISE

Alleluia! Jesus, we yield ourselves to Your purposes. Lord, we thank You that our present struggles, therefore our future achievements, are in Your will.

Father, I thank You for the grace to endure. I thank You for the strength to make it. I thank You for the time of trial, Lord, the time of testing. I thank You, Lord, for I know Your will is going to be done.

We thank You, Lord Jesus! We love You, Lord Jesus! Do Your work in our hearts today.

LETTING GO OF BITTERNESS

Some people blame God for their sufferings and misfortunes. We need to trust His wisdom. Understand that He is Wisdom; He's All-Wise. He knows all about us: our emotional makeup, our bodies, and our abilities. He knows how much we can take. He will never give us more than we can bear.

"Lord, I don't like the way I look. I don't like the way You made me." He made us as we are for a purpose. His glory will shine forth, and His glory shall be revealed.

If we have anything in our hearts that should not be there, we are to let God have His way in it. We are to let God do it. He will do it! Alleluia!

STUDY QUESTIONS CHAPTER 13

1. Our delight should be in the _____.

2. If we spend time in the Father's Presence, after awhile, we will simply _____ what God will like and what He won't.

3. _____ and _____ arrive for the Word's sake.

4. Determination is "understanding that our present _____ are preparing us for our future _____."

5. Meditation is simply "_____" God's promises.

6. When we start _____ on the Lord day and night, we will become like the person in Psalms 1, verse 3.

7. We are _____ and not cast down.

8. We are assured that we will bear fruit in our _____.

9. If we walk in God's principles, we will be as an evergreen tree - the foliage will always be there.

10. God knows how much we can take. He will never give us more than we can _____.

CHAPTER 14

Psalm means "a book of praise." We know that some of the psalms were written by David, but Psalms 1 and 2 are of unknown authorship. The book of Psalms is not only historic, it is also prophetic. Since we are in a prophetic move of God, the Psalms have special words for those with an ear to hear.

A few years ago, the prophetic word proclaimed the changing of the guard within the church. This word is already being manifested. The church is not getting weaker and weaker as some might think, but rather, it is getting stronger and stronger. We are to count the trials and testings of the church as a blessing. Persecution always brings multiplication. Every time Israel was persecuted, they multiplied. If we are going through persecution, we are being prepared for multiplication.

"Lord, I welcome the persecution that you appoint for my life."
Psalms 2, reads:

"WHY do the heathen rage, and the people imagine a vain thing?
The kings of the earth set themselves, and the rulers take counsel together, against the LORD, and against his anointed, saying, Let us break their bands asunder, and cast away their cords from us. He that sitteth in the heavens shall laugh: the Lord shall have them in derision. Then shall he speak unto them in his wrath, and vex them in his sore displeasure. Yet have I set my king upon my holy hill of Zion. I will declare the decree: the LORD hath said unto me, Thou art my Son; this day have I begotten thee. Ask of me,

and I shall give thee the heathen for thine inheritance, and the uttermost parts of the earth for thy possession. Thou shalt break them with a rod of iron; thou shalt dash them in pieces like a potter's vessel. Be wise now therefore, O ye kings: be instructed, ye judges of the earth. Serve the LORD with fear, and rejoice with trembling. Kiss the Son, lest he be angry, and ye perish from the way, when his wrath is kindled but a little. Blessed are all they that put their trust in him."

THE REACTION OF THE HEATHEN

Heathen means "a godless nation or a godless people." Anyone who does not have God in their life is a heathen. The Kingdom of God does not exist in their midst. If the Kingdom of Light is not there, then the kingdom of darkness and satan is there. The kingdom of darkness or satan operates not by the principle of obedience, but by the principle of disobedience or rebellion. Thus, the Scriptures tell us that obedience is better than sacrifice. Anything that is disobedient is as the sin of witchcraft.

CONFLICT

Rage, in verse 1 of the Psalms, refers to "anger, fury or a violent type of anger." Anytime the Kingdom of God comes face to face with the kingdom of satan, there is going to be conflict. Sometimes people come to the Lord and say, "I don't know what happened since I came to the Lord. My family treats me so differently! We had such a good relationship before I got saved. I don't know if this is worth it. Things seemed be better at home before I got saved."

The moment light comes in contact with darkness, there is conflict. If Christians claim people of the world as their best friends, there is a problem. There is something wrong. If we have fellowship with non-christians, our lives should either convict them, making them uncomfortable in our presence, or provoke them to come into the knowledge of God.

That doesn't mean preaching. We are a living epistle. If we truly represent God's Kingdom, when they are with us, they will notice something different about us. Our lifestyle alone will convict them. Why? The Kingdom of God has come into their midst. The Holy Spirit convicts.

VAIN MEDITATION VERSUS FRUITFUL MEDITATION

Vain imagination or vain meditation refers to "meditation without force, meditation which is fruitless without value." Some common examples are: worry (because it is fruitless and does not produce after the life of Christ); meditation on our checkbooks or

budgets; fretting, and talking to ourselves about things not of God. Vain meditation has no force and is without power, for power comes from God and His Word.
Fruitful imagination can sometimes be compared to the action of a cow chewing its cud. Some animals, notably the cow, chew their cud. Cows have four stomachs. They chew their food, regurgitate it, and start chewing what they regurgitated again. It is the regurgitated, re-eaten food which nourishes the cow.

The Holy Spirit will bring a thought to us, perhaps a prophetic word. We might chew on it for awhile, then perhaps try to move away from the full truth or realization of what it means. Suddenly, God will cause that word to regurgitate. It comes back to mind. We might say, "Wow! I didn't realize all that God was saying to me!"

God is bringing many of us to a place of fruitful meditation. His returning to our minds even things which He spoke to us many years ago. Perhaps years ago, God spoke some things in your life that seemed utterly impossible at that time. Now, you see yourself walking in those things. I have certainly seen this in my own life. There were words spoken over my family and I that were totally impossible when they were uttered. Now, I am seeing how God is bringing them forth into fulfillment.

God is causing all of His people to find their purpose in Him. At times, God likes to lead us as a blind man to places which are unfamiliar to us. We are going to know God's purpose, and we are going to see that God has established us and set us as stones in His temple.

GOD'S WORD - THE SOURCE FOR FRUITFUL MEDITATION

The Word is like an incorruptible seed. We do not have to teach a seed what it is supposed to do. Imagine giving a instructions to a seed: "You have to put down your roots; now you have to start pushing up from the ground, ..." etc. A seed has within itself the power and potential to reproduce after its kind, if it is planted in the proper soil and correct environment.

If we continue to let the seed of God's Word be planted in our lives, the seed will fall to the ground and die. We'll hear what God's will is. For instance, I walk in wealth so that I can establish His covenant. The moment we begin to claim that, our financial situation will begin to look terrible. The seed must die before the plant can come forth for harvest.

When we come to the Lord, we may tell Him that we will give Him everything, yet, we still hold on to a few things. For many of us, it is our finances. God wants to make us managers of what He places into our keeping. He wants to teach us stewardship. I recall one day speaking to the Lord about my need for clothing. "Lord, I am going out to minister. I need suits, shirts, and shoes." The Lord spoke to me and said, "Bernard, I will not bless your wardrobe until you learn to take care of those things which I have placed in your keeping already." Perhaps we haven't walked in the treasure that God has ordained for us because we haven't taken care of the small things He has placed in our care. Therefore, He cannot make us rulers over the many things.

A Vain Imagination is a Purpose Which Comes to Naught. Whenever we have a vain imagination, it will not result in fruit or life.

REACTING TO KINGS AND RULERS

Kings represent governmental authority and are rulers over nations. The Word of God says that "the heart of the king is in the hand of the Lord." How many of us really believe that? Do we believe that the heart of our boss is in the hand of the Lord? Many of us don't doubt the power of God, we doubt God's willingness. "Yes, I know that God can do anything, but is He willing to do something for me?"

My God is both able and willing. The heart of the king is truly in God's hand. He can change his heart just as He changes the course or path of a river. If we want to change the direction of a river's flow, we need only to put rocks in its path. Water takes the path of least resistance. God knows how to get the attention of the unsaved person in authority who may be disturbing or plaguing us. Their hearts are as rivers of water. All He has to do is place stumbling blocks in front of them.

As God applies pressure on authority figures over us, they will, at first, surely come against us. We, too, will feel the pressure as God deals with them. God has a way of turning and changing the hearts of men and women to bring them into His purpose and His order.

Rulers are authorities who are under kings. God is all authority; they are delegated authorities under Him. God has a way of bringing everything into His purpose.

BREAKING THE BAND AND CASTING AWAY THE CORD

Satan hates the Lord's anointed. Each of us who truly profess Jesus as Lord can say, "I am the anointed of God." Why does satan have such hatred of God's anointed? They represent the seed of God. The seed of the serpent is still coming against the seed of the woman. From the time of Adam and Eve, satan has been trying to destroy the Godly seed.

THE MEN ARE TO RISE UP

Now is the time for men to rise up and become the spiritual leaders of their households. the teaching and instruction shouldn't be left to the women. God did not tell Abraham, "Go tell Sarah to teach your children, and your children's children." Abraham was to be their teacher.

A men's manual I was reading contained a powerful teaching. A father's ministry does not end when his children become grown. It continues to his children's children. The stability of a family depends upon the stability of the grandfather. God is raising up many Godly generations.

If people haven't experienced Godly parenting and grandparenting, God wants to raise up men to be the first generation of Godly fathers and grandfathers in their families. They will the be able to give Godly impartation to their children and their grandchildren.

We were at a presbytery in upstate New York near the Canadian border. A couple I'd never met came up with their two little girls. We prophesied over the father and told him to lay hands on his daughters' bellies. The Lord began to prophesy saying, "Thou shalt be one. Thou shalt not only prophesy over thy children, but over thy children's children. Begin to speak the Word of the Lord in their lives and bring release." What happened was such a blessing. In the church that day were not only the daughter's grandfather, but also the great-grandfather. Five generations of that family were represented in that church. Imagine being in church with your children, grandchildren and great-grandchildren.

It is not God's will for children to be spread all over the continent away from their parents. That's a judgment of God. One of the things said in Deuteronomy chapter 28, verses 15 and 32 is:

"But it shall come to pass, if thou wilt not hearken unto the voice of the LORD thy God ...

"Thy sons and thy daughters shall be given unto another people, and thine eyes shall

look, and fail with longing for them all the day long:"

Separation from their children was a punishment to the Israelites because of their disobedience. I've been in places where the mother goes to one church, the children to another, and the father to another. The children have no stable church home. That's an abomination. God is going to bring families to church together, and keep them together in church for three and four generations. This will start to happen as we become people of covenant.

THE GOVERNMENT OF GOD

The wicked conspire to break the bands and cast away the cords of God's anointed. Those in the world often refuse to be under any kind of government, most especially the government of God. They want to be children of death. They cannot or will not endure the yoke of the Lord and the yoke of His anointed. The bands have to do with their consciousness. They do not want to know and understand the things of God. The cords have to do with the commandments. They do not want to bring their actions in line with God's laws and principles.

In ancient biblical times, cords were used to hold prisoners in bondage. In our nation today, people do not want to hear Godly principles. They are saying, "Let us break the band and cords of God's anointed ones. Listen to us. Your parents were born in the older generation. What they are teaching you is from the past. Don't listen to them."

THE ROD OF IRON

God has a mild way of dealing with people. He also has a time when He deals with them with the rod of iron. "Rod", refers to His authority. "Iron", speaks of the immutability of His Word. There comes a time where there is placed a demand upon us for obedience and submission to God's authority, rather than the unacceptable sacrifice proceeding from a heart of rebellion. How is a parent supposed to respond to open defiance by their children? Chastisement, punishment and restraint are absolutely necessary. Our Heavenly Father must respond to our disobedience with chastisement motivated by love that will help us to grow in grace and the knowledge of Him.

> "... *My son, despise not thou the chastening of the Lord, nor faint when thou art rebuked of him: For whom the Lord loveth he chasteneth, and scourgeth every son whom he receiveth. If ye endure chastening, God dealeth with you as with sons; for what son is he whom the father chaseneth not?" Hebrews 12:5-7*

God's desire is for a people that would understand the importance of obedience issuing from a heart that is in submission to His Word. This is truly the highest praise we can offer unto the Lord; our lives permeated with the sweet smelling fragrance of obedience. Not long ago, parents were routinely taught by pediatricians and child psychologists that it was very wrong to strike their children. They were told that children should be free, without any restrictions or bondage. What did this type of thinking produce? A generation of rebels who didn't understand restrictions or boundaries and did what was right in their own eyes.

BREAKING AWAY THE BANDS AND THE CORDS

The world isn't interested in bands and cords. We say that a man should be the husband of one wife and the world says, "Try out sex. Before you marry someone, live with her for awhile." They say it is fine to tell children that they should not indulge in premarital sex. But, just in case, be sure to introduce them to condoms.

Prayer has been removed from public schools. Children are told: "Be your own person." If a teacher or child mentions God or Jesus, he or she is persecuted within the school system. When I was in school, we talked about Jesus and preached Jesus in the hallways.

What is being taught is against the principles of God. What is being declared in the school system is, "Let us break their bands asunder; let us break their cords. We don't want restrictions anymore. We want to do what we think is right in our own eyes." There's deceptive talk about "safe sex," promoting "deceptive contraceptives" as the ultimate license for ungodly behavior. The only place to experience safe sex is in the marriage bed. Marriage and the marriage bed is honorable. Anything done outside of the marriage bed is defiled.

God is beginning to judge these things. The world would break the bands asunder. The world would stand in defiance of the government of God, but when you go beyond boundaries, you have to be willing to reap the consequences.

GOD'S REACTION

The laughter of the Lord is as the laughter at a company of fools. He holds those in the world and all of their attempts at defiance in derision. When God laughs, it is a form of judgment. Sometimes, laughter is a type of mocking. When God laughs, things happen. Often, when prophecies have come forth, I have heard the laughter of the Lord telling me how He is going to confound the wicked and turn their devices into naught.

Scripture records several people who laughed. In Genesis chapter 17, verse 17, we read:

"Then Abraham fell upon his face, and laughed, and said in his heart, Shall a child be born unto him that is an hundred years old? and shall Sarah, that is ninety years old, bear?" And again in Genesis chapter 18, verses 12-14, the laughter continues: "Therefore Sarah laughed within herself, saying, After I am waxed old shall I have pleasure, my lord being old also? And the LORD said unto Abraham, Wherefore did Sarah laugh, saying, Shall I of a surety bear a child, which am old? Is any thing too hard for the LORD? At the time appointed I will return unto thee, according to the time of life, and Sarah shall have a son."

The laughter of Sarah and Abraham should be a reminder and a lesson. The things we say we will never do the places we say we will never go are precisely the things we will do and precisely the places where God will send us.

Similarly, the people we say we will never deal with will be the very ones to which God will send us. Look at Saul. He was a devout Jew. Peter was a devout Jew also. The Jews of that day bore an intense hatred for the Gentiles. Yet, God sent them to the Gentiles.

The very people about whom we say, "Lord, I can't stand them. I don't want anything to do with them!" They are the ones to which God will send us and ask us to share Jesus. God is going to have His way in our lives - sometimes whether we like it or not. God knows how to take stones and place them in the river, causing us to be rerouted. How many of us have been rerouted even in the last year or two? God will change our direction. He will put circumstances in our path to cause us to go where He wants us to go. Often, we won't understand how we got there, but we'll know it's all of God! The Scripture tells us that God will mimic the wicked and hold them in derision. He knows that all of their devices are coming to naught.

THE SPOKEN WORD TO THE WICKED

When the Lord speaks, something is done. When He speaks against the wicked in anger, they will be undone. God will speak after a time. He will give the wicked time and space in which to repent.

Even in Genesis, we read how God approached Adam, giving him space to repent. God knew what Adam had done, yet He didn't confront him directly. Adam blamed God and others, "... the woman whom thou gavest to be with me, she gave me of the tree, and I did eat." (Genesis 3:12). Notice Adam was telling God, "If you hadn't given me Eve, then none of this would have happened. It's not my fault. It's your fault." Don't we do the same thing? "Lord, you know I would have been a better christian if you had saved my husband (wife) years ago. I could have done so much more for You."

Notice, too, how Eve did exactly the same as Adam, except she blamed the serpent. "... And the woman said, the serpent beguiled me, and I did eat." (Genesis 3:13). In a sense she was telling God, "the devil made me do it."

We, too, are quick to "pass the buck." We are very reluctant to simply say, "Lord, I sinned. I did something wrong. Forgive me." We have so many ways to justify ourselves: "Listen Lord, this happened because of ..." All of this is the nature of Adam. The Bible says, "He that covereth his sins shall not prosper: but whoso confesseth and forsaketh them shall have mercy" (Proverbs 28:13). If we are not prospering, could it be that we, like Adam or Eve, are hiding behind our aprons made of fig leaves?

When God speaks in verse 5 of Psalms 2, it refers not so much to words, but to actions. To someone badly in debt, what speaks may be a huge stack of unpaid bills, sleepless nights worrying, and notices from collection agencies. To a person who is careless about proper care of their body, the wordless statement might come from headaches, fatigue, weakened reflexes or dizziness. Divorce papers, children attempting suicide or a foreclosure on a home, can all be wordless statements. That's all saying something. "It is time for a change. It is time to repent of sin. It is time to look to the Lord your God as the answer."

Our bodies will often give us signals. The Holy Ghost will tell us to stop eating a certain food, often one we especially like. We may then be someplace where that is the main course. Too often we'll say, "I'll just bless the food and eat it. It will be all right just this once." If we ignore the laws and signals, we go against God's boundaries and limitations. We fail to understand God's purposes. If we do this, we are going to have problems somewhere down the line.

CHRIST DOES RULE
When God speaks to the wicked, one thing He will establish is that Christ does rule. He does reign. He sits as King. God has established the church. "... upon this rock I will build my church". Who is building the church? God! Notice that we are not to build the church. Furthermore, the gates of hell will not be able to prevail against the church. The church will be victorious because Christ reigns in the church as King.

DECLARING THE DECREE
The decree is a mystery - the mystery of the Son who was in the Father from the beginning. The word Son denotes relationship. Jesus Christ was in the bosom of the Father at the moment of creation. When the Father spoke the word, Jesus - the Word - went into action. When God said, "Let there be light," He was saying, "Once again, let Me be in the earth." God is Light. He was once again coming in the earth.

EXALTING THE KING
Jesus' commission was received from the Father. Jesus was set as Head of the Church. The body does not do anything apart from the head.

AS FOR THE INHERITANCE OF THE UNGODLY

Verse 8 of Psalms 2 says that the Lord will give us the heathen for an inheritance. The wealth of the wicked is stored up for us. (See Proverbs 13:22.) A man of wisdom and understanding is needed to draw it out. It will be a good thing when the church loses its tax exempt status. The church has been in a tax exempt status of: "non-profit." The church hasn't been profitable to the world, it hasn't been profitable to the people, and it hasn't been profitable to the nation.

We will be blessed when that status is taken away. For the scripture says, "But thou shalt remember the LORD thy God: for it is he that giveth thee power to get wealth." (Deuteronomy 8:18). God will teach His children how to prosper.

THE MEEK INHERITETH THE EARTH

Psalms 37:11 says:

> *"But the meek shall inherit the earth; and shall delight themselves in the abundance of peace."*

Numbers 12:3 says:

> *"(Now the man Moses was very meek, above all the men which were upon the face of the earth.)"*

Meekness is an interesting word. It means "patience, submission to bear what cannot be avoided." There are times when we might feel like disappearing from a situation, yet we know and obey the command of God to stay and see it through to the end. Patience is then having her perfect work in us.

The degree of a person's submission or meekness will be directly related to the degree of authority that God will cause that person to come into here on earth. If we are being oppressed, we need to stand (perhaps gritting our teeth) and say, "Lord, I thank You that my inheritance is coming." If we are wondering when a particular pressure will ever let up, we need to lift our hands to the Lord and say, "Father, I just thank You. You are preparing me to take over this situation some day."

Whatever we do not have dominion over, it will have dominion over us. God is preparing and raising us up as men and women who can deal with things and conquer that which has been as thorns in our flesh.

GOD'S LOVE

Love is not an emotion. It isn't someone coming up to us, embracing and saying, "I love you." Love is God. God is Love. If Jesus were here on earth today and He overturned the tables in the church, many would say, "That's not love!" Yet, Jesus was the very expression of Love.

I have a new definition of love. Love is boldness in action when we are moving in God's way and will. I believe that David was walking in love when he was cutting off the head of the giant Goliath. He was moving in God. I believe Samson was moving in love when he was defeating the enemies of Israel. He was moving in God.

Love never fails. Why? Because God never fails. Jesus walked in love to such a degree that even when His enemies wanted to come at Him to destroy Him, He just walked right through the midst of them. (See Luke 4:30.) That's the love of God. John, the revelator, was the apostle of love. They threw him in boiling oil, yet they couldn't kill him. Love never fails.

WISDOM AND JUDGMENT OF THE KINGS

"The fear of the Lord is the beginning of knowledge:" (Proverbs 1:7). Wisdom and judgment of kings should begin in the fear of the Lord and the reverence of the Lord. Submission to the Son is also needed.

In Psalms 2, we see reference to kissing the Son. In Old Testament times, among idolaters in India and Arabia, kissing was an act of worship. Kissing was also used as a token of reconciliation. When we kiss Jesus, we are reconciling ourselves with Him. To kiss the Son means to pay homage to Him, for He is the object of our worship.

STUDY QUESTIONS CHAPTER 14

1. _____ means "a book of praise."

2. A _____ is "a nation or nations, or a godless nation, or a godless people."

3. A _____ is a purpose which comes to naught.

4. Many of us don't doubt the power of God; we doubt God's _____ .

5. Now is the time for men to rise up and become the _____ of their households.

6. The wicked conspire to break the _____ and cast away the _____ of God's anointed.

7. Scripture tells us that God will mimic the _____ and hold them in derision.

8. We are quick to " _____ ." This is the nature of Adam.

9. _____ means "patience, submission to bear what cannot be avoided."

10. A new definition of _____ is boldness in action, when we are moving in God's way and His will.

CHAPTER 15

Many Christians question the legality and purpose of the ministry of dance in the House of the Lord. Perhaps they have been taught that all dance is sinful or a manifestation of soulish desires. Others may simply react to the fact that dance is unfamiliar and, therefore, warrants their suspicion. Yet, according to the Scriptures, dance is a viable ministry of expression that God has planted in the House of the Lord.

THE MEANING OF DANCE

Dance is simply rhythmic stepping or movements coordinated to the beat of music. It is patterned movements. Whatever the regenerated believer has experienced in his or her inner person, that experience should be expressed and brought forth in the outer man. The dance of the unregenerate, those that are alienated from God, is an expression of what is transpiring in their inner man. Their dance reflects the energies and desires of the soul, often which is accompanying lusts and frustrations. Their spirit is not one with Christ, and the holiness of God is not reflected in any of their artistic creations. Thus, their dance movements are filled with ungodly enticing movements.

The dance of the Spirit-filled believer reflect God, His Kingdom and His Mightiness. It also directs attention towards what God is saying, and the dance of the Lord will be an exact expression of the communion between the dancer's spirit and God. The dancer is able to portray that which they are receiving from God, and communicate it to the congregation, whether it be a dance of rejoicing, a dance of warfare, a dance of travail or a prophetic dance.

The Scripture cites many instances of dance. In Genesis 1:2, it says "... the spirit of God moved upon the face of the waters ..." I believe that the Spirit of God literally danced over the face of the deep. He moved according to a pattern. He danced a dance that brought order out of chaos, and prepared the earth to hear the instructions of the Lord.

Through movement, one can express what cannot be verbally articulated. Dance can also stimulate an emotional release. When we are dancing before the Lord, we may not be just breaking strongholds in the realm of the Spirit, but we may also be breaking strongholds in our own personal lives as well. For many of us, our early christian walk was marked with stiffness and an inability to move in the House of the Lord. We may have seen others rejoicing in God, but there we were, frozen in place, uncomfortable and afraid to move lest anyone would notice our presence. Some of us may have thought that movement just "didn't belong" in church. Therefore, we would view anyone that would dare to move about as a "fanatic" or "extremist." Yet, as we delve into the Word of God, we find that David, the king of Israel, danced and praised God. The Scripture says that David was "a man after God's own heart." So, the inevitable question demands an answer - what was it that distinguished David as being a man after God's own heart? The realization will begin to take root as we discover that David was a man of expression; his entire being, (spirit, soul and body), was given over to express worship unto the Lord.

The psalmist testifies to the delivering power of dance in Psalms 30:11, "Thou hast turned for me my mourning into dancing ..." When we move in an attitude of praise and worship during our times of grief and agitation, and freely offer our sacrifice of praise, God will begin to bring down strongholds. We begin to experience a new degree of freedom. Though the enemy would like to put our spirits in chains and in bondage, dance is a weapon that God has given us to express ourselves before Him, and He will bring deliverance into our lives.

Zephaniah chapter 3, verse 17, says:

> *"The LORD thy God in the midst of thee is mighty; he will save, he will rejoice over thee with joy; he will rest in his love, he will joy over thee with singing."*

He will joy over thee with singing" literally means God will dance over thee with a shout of triumph! Isn't that exciting? In spite of our situations, our pain, our afflictions, our difficulties, and our circumstances, God is in our midst, and He is mighty! Often, we don't really believe that God is truly mighty! Honestly, have you ever looked at a problem and thought, "This is impossible even for God?" The good news is that God is not only mighty, He is ALL MIGHTY!! He has all the might, power and ability to do whatever needs to be done. He will save (sozo); He will cleanse, and bring salvation to every area of our lives. Not only will God save us from our sins, but He will also save and preserve us in our circumstances.

I used to watch my mother and grandmother make preserves. They would get some peaches or pears and boil them, then they would put them in canning jars which had been boiled clean. They would make sure no air bubbles were in the jars and then seal them. The preserves could then be kept for years without spoiling. Many of us have already experienced and are still experiencing His preservation in our lives. God sets a seal upon us to keep us in our circumstances so that we will not be spoiled by what is happening around us.

Every time satan comes forward to accuse us to God, He just begins to spin with joy, saying, "That's My son!" or "That's My daughter! My children have been bought with a price!"

The world is discovering the potential of power in the dance. Doctors are recommending dance as therapy for psychological and physiological problems. After studying a patient's gestures and walking patterns, the doctor then choreographs certain dance steps that will help alleviate the various stresses that are affecting the patient. There are psychological case studies that show how, over a period of time, dance therapy can help correct certain aberrant personalities. The use and documentation of such therapy goes back to the 1940's.

DANCE - ITS PRESENT AND HISTORICAL RELATIONSHIP TO THE BELIEVER
DANCE HAS BEEN USED THROUGHOUT HISTORY

It has been used to acknowledge the elements and powers that man respected as gods. Each culture has acknowledged war, love, acts of strength, food, health and worship in their dances. Many of these dances followed the style of mime or interpretive dance. The belief that dance had power to invoke the power of the god intervene in circumstances is a pattern in many cultures and countries. A rain dance beseeched the gods to send rain upon the earth. Dance was performed before going to war. Many danced during the time of harvest in thanksgiving for the blessings of food they received.
There is a valuable principle here. We can see that ancient civilizations, which did not have the Word of God and were walking far light than we do today, proclaimed their victory in dance before they faced their adversaries.

In Hebrews chapter 11, verse 1, we read:

> "... *faith is the substance of things hoped for, the evidence of things not seen."*

There are many things that we won't be able to see with our natural eye, yet their reality is not to be denied. The faith of the Lord will uphold us, and will be the very ground support for our lives. Sometimes, as we're going through situations, we will hear the Lord telling us, "All is well." As our physical eyes focus on the signs before us, it becomes difficult to determine truth if we judge things solely by what our natural senses perceive. Yet, after emerging from the midst of the trial, we are inevitably amazed at the God-given ability to survive a difficult situation wrapped in a cocoon of the Word of the Lord.

Dance, as an expression used in our devotional time before the Lord, can bring the release that is necessary to embrace the truth of God's Word when everything around us is contrary to what we know is the truth. We need to allow our entire physical body, soul and spirit to be involved in declaring the truth in the face of our enemies; fear and doubt. As we dance before the Lord, our faith begins to build, and our receptivity increases to believe God's Word.

THE MINISTRY OF DANCE

The Hebrew word "mekholaw" means "a dance company or round dance; to dance or to whirl in a circular motion or to twist."

In Exodus chapter 15, verse 20, we read:

> "*And Miriam the prophetess, the sister of Aaron, took a timbrel in her hand; and all the women went out after her with timbrels and with dances."*

This is the first mention of a timbrel in the Scriptures. It's possible that the Israelites took the timbrel or drum out of Egypt. It came with them out of Africa. God is going to bring a variety of instruments into the church, some of them having never been seen before. People will go overseas on missionary trips and bring back new and unusual musical instruments to be dedicated and used in God's House to make a joyful noise unto the Lord.

In Exodus chapter 15, verse 21, we read:

> "*And Miriam answered them, Sing ye to the LORD, for he hath triumphed gloriously; the horse and his rider hath he thrown into the sea."*

Evidently, Miriam was leading a dance company of women. The women went out after her with timbrels in their hands. They were following after the order of Miriam. Once again, God is a God of order. As they were dancing, they were singing in choruses answering one another, proclaiming the works of God.

DANCE COMPANIES

The dance companies within the House of the Lord are called to stand and proclaim the works and attributes of God and demonstrate them in the midst of the congregation. They are able to cause the people to visualize that which God is doing and saying, and they help usher the congregation into higher realms of praise and worship. The closer the Word of God comes to being made a reality in our lives, the stronger our faith will become.

In Romans chapter 10, verse 17, we read:

"... faith cometh by hearing, and hearing by the word of God."

When we examine the Greek word "hearing," akoe or akouo, its definition, besides the ability of the natural physical ear to hear, also includes the word "audience," which carries the implication of acts of demonstration performed before a group of people that is heard and seen. Faith will arise as your understanding is enhanced by that which you hear and see. The ministry of dance, as well as other artistic modes such as drama, mime, art, puppetry, etc., are all ordained of God as avenues to build faith in His people.

In the Song of Solomon, chapter 6, verse 13, we read:

"Return, return, O Shulamite; return, return, that we may look upon thee. What will ye

see in the Shulamite? As it were the company of two armies."

The original Hebrew translation of the word "Shulamite" is "a company of dancers" or "a dance company." Therefore, the question that is actually being asked is, "What will ye see in the dance company? As it were, a company of two armies." The dance companies are anointed to do warfare in the realm of the Spirit. They prophesy and proclaim the Word of the Lord as a standard in the face of the enemy.

The dance company is to be aligned as an army in the House of the Lord. Each member is to be a worshipper of the Lord Jesus Christ. There is an appointed rank and file to the order of the dancers, and there is one appointed leader. Their attire will also portray a vision of holiness and order in the House of the Lord. Their outfits will be uniform with one another, reflecting the beauty of holiness. A dance company ministers as part of a team, having oneness of mind, worshipping the Lord together.

DANCE AND PROPHESY

In 1 Samuel 18:6-8, we find a company of dancers that are prophesying of Saul and David's victories; they proclaimed "Saul hath slain his thousands, David his ten thousands." At that time, David did not have ten thousand victories, he had only battled the lion, the bear and Goliath.

Here is an important lesson to be learned as we examine the life and calling of David. When the prophet Samuel anointed David to be king over Israel, David did not proclaim the news of his anointing and placement by God. Neither did he attempt to displace Saul and force his assumption of the throne. But rather, he continued doing what he was already doing and let the anointing oil "settle in."

Most of us have difficulty allowing the anointing to settle in. Our egos cause us to desire immediate recognition for who and what we are in God. Uncontrolled, this impulse can cause us to abort the very thing that God desired to build; for we move impetuously and leave the church to allow our "anointing" to flow. Many of us have never received the fullness of the anointing of God in our lives, for we moved from the appointed place of preparation into an area of spiritual desolation.

God may anoint you as a prophet while you are a church musician, dancer, serving on the housekeeping team or as an office worker. When you've received His anointing, there are two things that can be done. (1) You can thank the Lord for His anointing and for the upcoming day of separation that will come in His time, or, (2) You can lay aside your duties and announce to the world, "I am going to prophesy," then depart from your post ill-equipped, frustrated and eventually deceived.

Premature attempts to ascend into your calling before your maturation results in stunted growth and an inability to walk in the fullness of the anointing that God has ordained for you to walk in. You will make a mess of the situation and fail to walk in your full calling. You will have missed your season of preparation.

Unfortunately, the church is plagued by a myriad of individuals that have missed their time of preparation. This condition manifests itself in weak leadership, erroneous teaching, stunted growth, and imitative ministry. When David volunteered to fight Goliath, Saul gave David his armor. Yet, David could not function while wearing Saul's armor. We cannot fight a war with someone else's armor on. Many people are standing in places of ministry today ill-prepared, and they have developed into nothing more than echoes of another person. They lack a distinctive voice of their own. God desires to raise His ministers up as a voice in the earth. His Word is to be engrafted into us to such a degree that it becomes a part of our very being, causing us to sound as a trumpet in the earth.

This is a condition, fueled by unbridled ambition, that afflicts many in the Body of Christ. However, it is also frequently found in the ministry of the worshipping arts. Individuals begin to sense the anointing of God as they minister. They feel that they are now ready to ascend into high places of ministry without completing the necessary time of preparation that God has ordained for their lives. Artistic temperament, when not subjected to the dealings of God, will usually adapt to the same pattern that caused Lucifer to lose his place of authority in the Kingdom of God. Pride, rebellion, delusion, self-exaltation, and unrestrained ambition will mark the place of worship that the artistic minister is called to stand in, and cause them to fall, experiencing a change in their name; even as Lucifer is now called satan. The light-bearer became the opponent; an enemy of God.

When we allow ourselves to lose the focus of our ministry and begin to desire adulation and praise from the hands of men, our ministry becomes corrupt. In like manner, our name changes also, for we cease being His light-bearers and join the company of those that oppose Him in the earth. That our gift or talent which has been dedicated and separated unto the Lord, is HOLY and must always be guarded to be kept in purity and holiness. We are never to allow impatience and eagerness to cause us to cast our pearls before swine; we are to understand the value of that which has been entrusted unto us, and submit to the nurturing of the Lord.

THE SELAH (DANCE AND MEDITATION)
The word, selah, is found frequently in the psalms, yet its exact meaning is a bit obscure. It refers to "a musical rest," or "a time of meditation." Occasionally, it is translated as "pause and think about it." It is surmised that possibly, while the musician played, as the selah was pronounced, it was a time that the dancers would interpret in dance what had been ministered by the psalmist in song. This dance, during a musical interlude, interpreted what the Spirit of the Lord was saying unto the congregation. Unfortunately, we have not seen this manifestation of the Spirit often in the House of the Lord. However, I believe that as the church walks in the restorative move of God, with fresh understanding and comprehension concerning the worshipping arts and their function in the House of the Lord, we will begin to experience, once again, dimensions of praise and worship that will incorporate those arts that were lost and restore them.

The selah is also more important than we realize. Many of our church services tend to pattern themselves without any type of rest or meditative time to absorb what has been said or demonstrated. Yet, as we explore the scriptures, everything in creation experiences a time of rest. The innate structure of music contains times of rest. God

Himself worked for six days and on the seventh He rested. Our society has influenced us to a point that we tend to work through the times that ought to be set apart as a time of rest. Many of us believe that if we aren't always doing something, we are not being spiritual enough. We need to experience the reality that there is a season for everything under the sun; a time to work and a time to rest.

THE DANCER AND THE CALL

The ministry of dance attracts much attention because of the fact that it must be gazed upon. Therefore, as with other areas of ministry, character development is essential for anointed ministry. Personal aspirations must be laid upon the altar of sacrifice, and the dancers must submit to the dealings of God in their lives. Unfortunately, many dancers succumb to the character weaknesses of jealousy and pride; becoming jealous of another's talent or prowess, and prideful of their own. When jealousy overtakes an individual, murder literally enters their heart, and they may act upon it physically or spiritually by spreading slanderous remarks which destroy other's perceptions of the targeted person's character. One instance is found when the dancers began to prophesy about Saul and David.

"And the women answered one another as they played, and said, Saul hath slain his thousands, and David his ten thousands. And Saul was very wroth, and the saying displeased him; and he said, They have ascribed unto David ten thousands, and to me they have ascribed but thousands: and what can he have more but the kingdom? And Saul eyed David from that day and forward." 1 Samuel 18:7-9

Often, there may be a dancer functioning on the dance team whose talent may exceed the others, or who may be especially anointed to minister their spirit unto the congregation and spark a response in the congregation on a level that the others are not anointed to do. Unless there is an understanding of rank and a death of personal ambition, (which will produce true submission to the sovereign will of God), jealousy will erupt. The jealous individual will begin to focus upon, magnify and project every weakness imaginable upon the person that triggers their jealousy. Jealousy comes as a response to an individual's insecurity. This is why, when functioning as part of a team, (and applicable to any aspect of ministry), one must have confidence in the sovereign appointments of God and understand that all promotion comes from Him.

As members of the Body of Christ, we must understand our boundaries of function as established by God. All authority comes from God, and it is He who decides the measure of rule that we are to function in. It is important to understand that the degree which we are in submission to God and to His delegated authorities determines the degree of our authority. We must also recognize that the boundaries were already established by God. Therefore, there is no need to feel rejected, slighted or inferior because you've compared your ministry to another's, and you feel that yours is found wanting. Comparison is dangerous because it causes evil thoughts to fester as poison in your heart, and in turn, produces the bitter fruit of competition to manifest in your behavior. Competition is self-inflicted torture; you are driven by feelings of insecurity and inferiority to constantly strive to be "the best." You can never attain a state of contentment because everything you do is never "good enough." You live with a mantle of criticism weighing heavily upon your shoulders. You are unable to express yourself in the arts because you are in bondage to your own fear of failure.

We must forever endeavor to move in the agape love of Jesus Christ, willing to see nothing but the good in one another and esteeming our brother or sister higher than ourselves. If we are truly esteeming them higher than ourselves, then we will truly rejoice at any elevation that comes into their lives, rather than feel personally threatened or slighted. This is how we will become immune to the carnal tendencies to react with the sin of jealousy, and worship as an overcomer.

DANCERS ARE APPOINTED

The leadership of the church should appoint the dancers because it is a ministry unto the Lord. When we attend church, you never hear anyone say, "Who would like to pastor the church today?" that is appointed by God. In like manner, the ministers of dance and music in the House of the Lord are to be appointed. Everyone cannot dance prophetically before the Lord in the congregation. The dancer should be appointed, for this is a holy ministry unto the Lord.

As in music or any other area of the arts, much time is given to the training and discipline necessary to perfect the talent. It is the same for dancers. They should be skilled and minister in a spirit of excellence, which requires training and practice. If someone really feels that they are called to the ministry of dance, they should enroll in a dance school and develop their talent and skill. Mundane ministry disrespects and dishonors God, who gave His best for us.

A lot of us tend to offer God our leftovers. If, for instance, we aspire to minister on Broadway, in the arena of the world system, we would be diligent to perfect our craft and audition in excellence. Why is it we feel that mediocrity is acceptable in the House of the Lord? If we truly believe God is calling us to a particular area of the arts, then we are to be good stewards of the talent which God has given and be diligent in studying to show ourselves approved. Let us cultivate dedication and honor in the House of the Lord.

Singers use their voices, orchestra members use their instruments, artists use their brushes, and dancers use their bodies. All are to display the beauty and purity of the Spirit. When we speak of appointing people to work within the church, most people react by saying, "That's bondage!" Why? Because most people resist the slightest evidence of true authority in action. Most people, unless the root of rebellion has been dealt with by the Spirit of the Lord, find authority distasteful and threatening to their liberty. This attitude breeds a critical spirit that constantly seeks and delights in finding flaws in the delegated authority. Yet, as we study the Scriptures, we find that order and authority is crucial in every aspect of the ministry, especially the arts. If we don't have the vision of the House, with corresponding submission and respect for the authorities that are over us, then we cannot effectively flow or minister before the Lord together.

It is always grossly evident when someone begins to minister out of order. Their music, dance, acting or whatever, though technically correct, tangibly transmits their rebellion. Therefore, it behooves all of us to allow the time of preparation necessary to develop mature christian character; thus, increasing our effectiveness in the demonstration of the Word of God.

STUDY QUESTIONS CHAPTER 15

1. _____ is simply rhythmic stepping or movements coordinated to the beat of music.

2. The dance of the Spirit-filled believer reflects _____ .

3. Dance is a _____ that God has given us to express ourselves before Him and bring _____ into our lives.

4. _____ means "a dance company or round dance, to dance or to whirl in a circular motion or to twist."

5. Faith will arise as your _____ is enhanced by what you _____ .

6. The dance company is to be aligned as an _____ in the House of the Lord.

7. Premature attempts to ascend into your calling before your maturation results in growth and an inability to walk in the fullness of the _____ that God has ordained for you to walk in.

8. Artistic temperament, when not subjected to the dealings of God, will usually adapt to the same pattern that caused Lucifer to lose his place of authority in the Kingdom of God. They are _____ .

9. If we don't have the vision of the House, with corresponding submission and respect for the authorities that are over us, then we cannot _____ before the Lord together.

CHAPTER I

1.   There were no study questions after chapter one; only questions for reflection.

CHAPTER 2

Reflections

1.   What are some specific things you can do to make your personal and corporate praise more thought-filled? Do several of these things and see how they affect our personal and corporate praise and worship.

   Suggestions
   In my personal praise I can:
   - a.   Set aside time each day to praise and worship the Lord.
   - b.   Praise the Lord in spite of how I feel.

2.   List the dimensions of praised mentioned in this chapter. Which one is least familiar to you? Discuss that dimension of praise and think of ways that it might be used in your personal or corporate praise and worship.
   - a. Sacrifice of Praise
   - b. Praise and Worship / Thought-filled act
   - c. Worship of God alone
   - d. Praise - a way of deliverance

3.   "When people see our lives, they see a poem. They see a statement of God." Do you know people whose lives are a statement of God? How is this true of your life? Begin to thank God for making your life His statement.

Personal Answer

4.   List three teachings of humanism with which you are personally familiar. Look up Scriptures that specifically come against these teachings. The do any or all of the following:
   - a. Write out one of the Scriptures. Post it in a prominent spot in your home. Memorize it.
   - b. Make a simple poster or banner based on one of the Scriptures. Display it in your home and or your church hall.
   - c. find a song based on one of the Scriptures. Sing it as you worship the Lord in your home or at the church.

   Suggestion
   Romans 3:23 - "Man is self-sufficient."
   Man is in control of his life and destiny - Proverbs 14:12; 16:25
   Man has caused himself to achieve honor and wisdom - Romans 12:3

CHAPTER 2 STUDY

1. The people of God should learn to love the Lord.
2. God wants to restore creativity to the Body of Christ.
3. David danced before the Lord. Even the priests had to be able to dance.
4. Praise is better than sacrifice.
5. The book of Revelation is not a book about the anti-Christ, but is the revelation of Jesus Christ.
6. What humanism teaches and what the humanist wants is your mind and your hands.
7. We need to progress to where our praise is of such a degree that our minds are continually on Him.
8. The Greek word for workmanship is "poiema" which means "a poem."
9. The Kingdom of God is at hand. It is here and now.
10. If we are going to be the Judah of God, we must become the praise of God.

CHAPTER 3

1. Satan realizes the value and importance of worship.
2. Seven is the number of completion and perfection.
3. Incense represents prayer, praise and worship.
4. There is a difference between the prayer of petition and the prayer of praise.
5. True prayer is only that which is lit by the fire of God.
6. There is a kind of prayer unctioned by a person's soul.
7. Jesus said, "I come quickly. My reward is with Me."
8. We are to move in the force and power of God to such a degree that we take the Kingdom of God for His glory.
9. As parents and pastors, we are to display to our children the glory and authority of God.
10. Praise will annihilate the works of the enemy.

CHAPTER 4

1. We're to move only with God's flow and His pattern.
2. Prayer unctioned by the Holy Spirit is a sweet smell in the Father's nostrils.
3. In the Bible, everything is a true statement; however, everything is not a statement of truth.
4. Prayer and praise create an atmosphere in which God can move.
5. Formula praise is an abomination in the Father's nostrils.
6. We must guard against too much familiarity with God's Presence.
7. When that which we build is not according to the pattern or plan or God, He won't dwell in it.
8. God has established local churches as places of feeding for His people.
9. The entire Old Testament, from Genesis to Malachi, was and is for the Church.
10. There is a time to put everything aside and simply worship the Lord.

CHAPTER 5

1. God wants to bring forth a people who will worship Him in Spirit and in truth.
2. Praise is to come from our innermost being.
3. Leah is hte first person to use the word "praise" (Judah) in the scriptures.
4. Complaining rejects the providence of God and renders praise to satan.
5. True praise is the sincere acknowledgement of worth, based upon one's real conviction.

CHAPTER 6

1. When we praise the Lord, our hand is in the neck of the enemy.
2. The enemy fights a praising people and tries to make them look silly or inferior.
3. Praise stills the enemy.
4. The very thing the enemy designed to destroy us can be the very thing which God will use to raise us up.
5. We need to praise God for Who He is and for His attributes.
6. Some people make the mistake of viewing God and satan as equal adversaries on opposing sides.
7. Lucifer was once known as the anointed cherub.
8. A viol is a stringed bow instrument, possibly having six strings.
9. Lucifer was a complete orchestra. When he fell, God made us to be worshippers, for we are taking the place of Lucifer.

CHAPTER 7

1. Every time satan sees us, he is reminded of the place from which he fell.
2. God wants a people who will meet their circumstances early by praising Him.
3. Music was originally created for the purposes of God.
4. When played under the anointing of God, an instrument can begin to prophesy.
5. Before someone can be a man or woman of authority, they must first be a man or woman under authority.
6. Samuel was the first one to establish a School of the Prophets and he used music to train up young prophets.
7. Music was and is vital in the School of the Prophets.
8. The psaltery is a 10-string harp; the tabret is a tambourine; and the pipe is a kind of flute.
9. There seems to be a relationship between music, instruments and prophecy.
10. A minstrel is one who "beats a tune with their fingers, playing upon a stringed instrument."
11. When the Lord inhabits the praise of Israel, He makes a throne upon the praises of His people.
12. A church that moves into worshipping God in spirit and truth will unseat satan.

CHAPTER 8
1. Webster's dictionary defines music as "the art or science of harmonic sounds."
2. The etymology or root meaning of a word often provides important clues to its meaning.
3. Even from the earliest times man created and had access to musical instruments.
4. The arts were formed out of the lineage of Cain.
5. Anointed music not only soothes, it also has the ability to bring or draw out the Word of the Lord.
6. The next move of God is coming on the wings of praise and worship.
7. Music is for work and warfare.
8. David understood firsthand that praise could soothe and curtail the rage of the enemy.
9. When in deep trouble, a wise person seeks out a prophet; someone with the Word of the Lord.
10. Our praise creates an atmosphere for the Father to set up His throne.

CHAPTER 9
1. Music will be a part of the occupation of those in heaven.
2. We truly need to understand that our ministry is not to one another, but to the Lord.
3. The word "Exodus" means "the way out."
4. One reason why so many people do not know how to praise God is because their leaders haven't told them or showed them how to do it.
5. The song of Moses was partially historically and partially prophetic, painting a glorious picture of the future.
6. Women can surely be leaders within the church.
7. The timbrel originated in Egypt, and was generally played by women.
8. There must be a call of the Lord upon the life of the musician.
9. Musicians and singers will once again usher in the powerful presence of God.
10. The chosen Old Testament musicians played three types of instruments: the psaler, harp, and cymbal.

CHAPTER 10
1. Prophetic songs can also be used as spiritual songs.
2. Clever, skilled musicians were chosen or picked out by the king and instructed in the songs of the Lord.
3. As we bring forth our song, there will be a liftfing of our burden and a lifting up of God's presence in our worship services.
4. Fear is the opposite of Faith.
5. If we lack understanding of the contract, (of our covenant with God) we will not know what we have a right to expect from God.
6. Circumcision was a sign of the covenant.
7. In a battle, it is essential that everyone knows how to be a joint that supplies.
8. When the priests went forward adorned in fine linen and wearing precious ornaments, they were making a statement to their enemies.

9. The Targums, a Jewish book, indicates that the ancient Israelites believed that angelic powers went into operation when they began to praise God.
10. After any spiritual battle we fight, we come out with prosperity.

CHAPTER 11

1. Todah praise means "to give thanks and praise for what God is going to do."
2. We, the church of Jesus Christ, too often put giving last and give from our leftovers.
3. Barak praise speaks of reverence.
4. Shabak praise is a loud praise.
5. Zamar praise is often done using stringed instruments.
6. Halel praise refers to praise which shines forth fearlessly and with foolish exuberance.
7. Tehillah praise differs from the other forms of praise in that while the other forms involve faith, this word implies that God has responded to that faith.
8. Hymns denote "songs of praise addressed to God."
9. A relationship must be vertical before it can be horizontal.
10. In toom many of our churches, we have a gathering of people, but no assembling.

CHAPTER 12

1. In praise, we can express ourselves to God.
2. Yadah praise refers to praise in the stretching forth of our hands.
3. The will of God on earth is not sickness, but health; not poverty, but prosperity.
4. A person should fast when God ordains and moves upon him or her to do so.
5. God will take the weak or foolish things to confound the mighty.
6. God wanted man to be in such a place that when He looked at man He would see Himself.
7. The degree of depth in our relationship with God will be the degree with which God deals with us.
8. Any time you're under pressure to make a decision, you will always make the wrong decision.
9. The Law of Dominion states, "Whatsoever I do not have dominion over, it has dominion over me."
10. The commission thus received in Genesis was for man to utilize, for his necessitites, the vast resources of the earth.

CHAPTER 13

1. Our delight should be in the Scriptures.
2. If we spend time in Father's presence, after a while, we will simply know what God will like and what He won't.
3. Persecution and affliction arrive for the Word's sake.
4. Determination is "understanding that our present struggles are preparing us for our future achievements."
5. Meditation is simply "worrying" God's promises.
6. When we start meditating on the Lord day and night, we will become like the person in

Psalms 1:3.

7. We are planted and not cast down.

8. We are assured that we will bear fruit in our proper season.

9. If we walk in God's principles, we will be as an evergreen tree -- the foliage will always be there.

10. God knows how much we can take. He will never give us more than we can bear.

CHAPTER 14

1. Psalm means a "book of prasie."

2. A heathen is "a godless nation" or a "godless people."

3. A vain imagination is a purpose which comes to naught.

4. Many of us don't doubt the power of God; we doubt God's willingness.

5. Now is the time for men to rise up and become the spiritual leaders of their house holds.

6. The wicked conspire to break the bands and cast away the cords of God's anointed.

7. Scripture tells us that God will mimic the wicked and hold them in derision.

8. We are quick to "pass the buck." This is the nature of Adam.

9. Meekness means "patience, submission to bear that which cannot be avoided."

10. A new definition of love is boldness in action when we are moving in God's way and His will.

CHAPTER 15

1. Dance is simply rhythmic stepping or movements coordinated to the beat of music.

2. The dance of the Spirit-filled believer reflects God, His Kingdom and his Mightiness.

3. Dance is a weapon that God has given us to express ourselves before Him and bring deliverance into our lives.

4. Mekholaw means "a dance company, or round dance or to whirl in a circular motion or to twist."

5. Faith will arise as your understanding is enhanced by what you see and hear.

6. The dance company is to be aligned as an army in the House of the Lord.

7. Premature attempts to ascend into your calling before your maturation results in stunted growth and an inability to walk in the fullness of the anointing that God has ordained for you to walk in.

8. Artistic temperament, when not subjected to the dealings of God, will usually adapt to the same pattern that caused Lucifer to lose his place of authority in the Kingdom of God. They are pride, rebellion, self-exaltation, and unrestrained ambition.

9. If we don't have the vision of the house with corresponding submission and respect for the authorities over us, then we cannot effectively flow or minister before the Lord together.

MINISTRIES

P.O. Box 270 • New York, NY 10008
Call (914) 351-7250
To Order by Phone

Name: _____

Address: _____

City: _____ State: _____ Zip Code: _____

Day Phone: _____ Evening Phone: _____

Grand Total: $_____ _ Chech / Money Order Enclosed _ Cash _ Credit Card

Credit Card #: _____ Exp. Date: _____

Signature: _____

**BOOKSTORES:
Call for
volume discounts!**

QTY	TITLE	EACH	TOTAL
	Mentoring: The Missing Link	$10	
	Mentoring: The Iconoclastic Approach to Development of Ministry	$10	
	The Mastery of Mentorship	$10	
	Servanthodd	$10	
	Spiritual Protocol	$20	
	The Spirit of the Oppressor	$10	
	The Spirit of Liberation	$10	
	His Color Was Black: A Race Attack	$10	
	Keys to Liberation	$10	
	The Power of the Dime	$10	
	The Power of Money	$10	
	The Achiever's Guide to Success	$10	
	Praise and Worship	$20	
	Breaking Soul Ties and Generational Curses	$10	
	Meditation: Key to New Horizons in God	$10	
	The Holy Spirit	$10	
	Prayer and Fasting	$10	
	The Joshua Generation	$10	
	The Making of the Dream	$10	
	Written Judgments Volume 1	$10	
	Written Judgments Volume 2	$10	
	Written Judgments Volume 3	$10	
	The Seed of Destiny	$10	
	Prophetic Genesis	$10	
	The Science of Prophecy	$10	
	School of the Prophets Volume 1	$50	
	School of the Prophets Volume 2	$50	
	School of the Prophets Volume 3 (new)	$50	
	The Science of Prophetic Leadership	$10	
	What Every Woman Should Know About Men	$10	
	Above All Things Get Wisdom	$1	
	Calling Forth The Men of Valor	$1	
	The Purpose of Tongues	$1	
	Keys to Your Success	$1	